ALAN HAYES

It's so
NATURAL™

HOUSE *book*

Angus&Robertson
An imprint of HarperCollins*Publishers*

**For everyone who is committed
to using our natural resources wisely**

Angus&Robertson
An imprint of HarperCollins*Publishers*, Australia

First published in Australia in 1997
by HarperCollins*Publishers* Pty Limited
ACN 009 913 517
A member of HarperCollins*Publishers* (Australia) Pty Limited Group

HarperCollins*Publishers*
25 Ryde Road, Pymble, Sydney NSW 2073, Australia
31 View Road, Glenfield, Auckland 10, New Zealand
77–85 Fulham Palace Road, London W6 8JB, United Kingdom
Hazelton Lanes, 55 Avenue Road, Suite 2900, Toronto, Ontario M5R 3L2
and 1995 Markham Road, Scarborough, Ontario M1B 5M8, Canada
10 East 53rd Street, New York NY 10032, USA

National Library of Australia Cataloguing-in-Publication data:

Hayes, Alan B. (Alan Bruce), 1949- .
The 'it's so natural' house book : how to conserve energy
and save money in and around your home.

ISBN 0 207 19077 1.

1. Dwellings – Energy conservation. I. Title.

644

Printed in Australia by Griffin Paperbacks on 79 gsm Bulky Paperback.

9 8 7 6 5 4 3 2 1   01 00 99 98 97

CONTENTS

INTRODUCTION

Today, almost everyone is feeling the energy pinch — the cost of utilities is rising and increasingly affecting our lives. Despite the prevailing use of non-renewable fuels to produce energy, and the negative impact it has on the earth's elements, we can as individuals take an active role in helping to alleviate this problem. By re-evaluating our day-to-day needs and modifying our household habits we can learn to conserve and use energy wisely.

As electricity is the most expensive form of energy, space heating and cooling your home can be extremely costly. Add to this the cost of providing domestic hot water and power consumption levels can soar. Yet by simply shading windows on a hot summer's day, fitting curtains with box pelmets and drawing them at night, and increasing insulation on hot water tanks, heat gain and loss can be greatly reduced. Beyond these simple solutions are many techniques, including correct and adequate house insulation, that will save energy, lower your fuel costs and increase your comfort levels.

A lot of conservation improvements may seem to have very little impact on day-to-day living, but in the long term will be of substantial benefit. Others may require a little habit modification but, by and large, to save energy is simply a matter of upgrading your house. Upgrading your house does not mean carrying out major alterations or extensions, but simply integrating energy-saving design. Of course, when building a new home, passive-solar and energy-saving design can be incorporated to maximise its effectiveness. Ideally, an energy-saving home would: be an elongated shape and face north (south in the northern hemisphere); have large windows on the north (south in the northern hemisphere) to receive winter sun and summer shade; have a concrete slab floor or internal brick walls to receive and store the sun's heat during the day in winter and maintain a cool climate in summer; have few, if any, windows on the east and west sides, and few windows on the south side (north in the northern hemisphere); and be weather-tight and well insulated.

Most of you, however, will not be starting from scratch by building a house, but will have to look at the most cost effective way in which you can modify your existing home. The most abundant, readily available source of energy is the sun. A clean and renewable resource, it bombards us daily with thousands of times more energy than we could possibly ever use. Energy from the sun can be used to generate electricity, for climate control (heating and cooling), and to heat water.

Generating electricity using solar energy may seem a little fanciful in densely populated urban areas. However, even a modest solar array (group of electric solar cells) could supply power for circulating fans, lights and some, if not all, electrically operated appliances. With solar cells there is no waste heat or pollution because no fuel is needed to produce electricity. A practical solution is to combine solar usage and power from the electricity grid — excess power from your solar array can be directed back into the grid, for which you will receive a credit against the power provided by your electricity supplier.

In urban areas, solar energy can be incorporated into most homes for cost effective residential heating and cooling. These types of systems operate on very basic principles and are simple and safe because of the low temperatures they operate within. They can be installed with relative ease and maintained by unskilled home owners.

An energy-efficient home will not only mean savings to you but also to the environment. This book is not about spending thousands of dollars on your home to implement dollar-saving systems to reduce energy usage. It is simply about incorporating sensible and effective ideas to cut down on excessive use of non-renewable energy, and using simple systems which take advantage of free solar energy. Obviously, some of the systems will require a certain amount of monetary outlay, but this will be balanced against eventual savings in lower fuel bills and less dependency on fossil fuels.

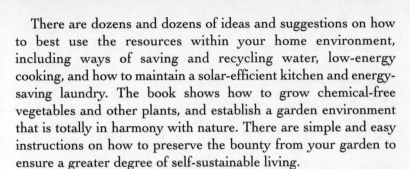

There are dozens and dozens of ideas and suggestions on how to best use the resources within your home environment, including ways of saving and recycling water, low-energy cooking, and how to maintain a solar-efficient kitchen and energy-saving laundry. The book shows how to grow chemical-free vegetables and other plants, and establish a garden environment that is totally in harmony with nature. There are simple and easy instructions on how to preserve the bounty from your garden to ensure a greater degree of self-sustainable living.

This book has been written to give you a better understanding of how to live simply, and simply live. Although it is important for all of us to work together globally, it is just as necessary to take stock on the home front. Environmentally friendly homes and habits must lead to a healthier planet, guaranteeing future generations the same joy and beauty we have been able to experience.

Alan Hayes

GETTING STARTED

The goal of the natural house is to conserve earth's precious resources, minimising the costs of running the household as well as the amount of harm it causes to the environment. While there are many ways you can both run an economical household and show your respect for the environment, if you're serious about minimising your use of non-renewable resources, the most fundamental step is to look at the structure of your house. Does it take full advantage of the most environmentally friendly resource known to humankind — the sun?

For many people, 'solar' means solar electricity and solar hot water systems. But these two important and economical uses of solar energy, which are discussed in Chapter 4, are not the only way that you can use the sun. By implementing a few simple passive-solar design principles, your house itself can become a solar energy collector.

ACTIVE AND PASSIVE SYSTEMS

Heating or cooling systems that rely on electricity to move warm or cool air, or water, around are known as active systems. Usually, active systems, such as air-conditioning units, are not cost effective because they consume a tremendous amount of energy for a relatively small output. Systems that do not use electricity but run instead on natural processes such as solar radiation and convection are called passive systems. Simplicity, effectiveness, minimal energy wastage and low running costs make passive heating and cooling systems an attractive and sensible choice.

However, in some cases it can be advantageous to combine an active system with passive-solar systems to make them more effective. This is especially so if all that is required is a low-amperage fan or pump that would use no more than one-tenth of the total electricity used by an active system.

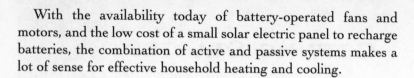

With the availability today of battery-operated fans and motors, and the low cost of a small solar electric panel to recharge batteries, the combination of active and passive systems makes a lot of sense for effective household heating and cooling.

THE INFLUENCE OF THE SUN

The sun is the earth's primary power plant and its daily delivery of energy affects and influences all climatic conditions. Its radiant energy provides warmth that is essential for all life to exist — it helps plants recycle carbon dioxide and soil nutrients to make oxygen.

It is this radiant energy that we can utilise to both warm and cool our homes, convert into electricity and use to warm our water, thus reducing our dependency on non-renewable and polluting energy sources.

The sun's energy is most concentrated when it strikes the earth directly perpendicular to its surface (0 degree angle of incidence). As the earth's surface tilts with the changing seasons the same amount of energy is spread over a large area and therefore less energy is received per unit of surface area. This is why in summer, when the sun is higher in the sky (and the angle of incidence is less), we experience warmer climatic conditions, and in winter, when the sun is lower in the sky (and the angle of incidence is greater), the weather is far cooler.

The angle of incidence is an important factor in understanding the earth–sun relationship where you live. For example, the closer you are to the equator, the higher the angle of the sun will be in both winter and summer, and the further you are from the equator, the lower the angle will be. This is an important factor when incorporating solar design into your home.

THE SUN IN YOUR PLACE

There are four basic elements that have a significant effect on human comfort: sunlight, temperature, humidity and wind. Our homes are designed to separate us from undesirable elements and provide us with as much comfort as possible.

Ideally, an elongated house running east to west, with living rooms and kitchen facing north (south in the northern hemisphere), will maximise living comfort. Large windows on that side, with overhanging eaves or pergolas will give shade from the high-angle summer sun and allow warmth from the lower-angle winter sun.

When buying a house, you'll find that many houses have not been built to maximise the benefits of a northern aspect (or southern in the northern hemisphere). Preferably, purchase a house that requires minimum renovation to receive plenty of northern light (southern in the northern hemisphere) but if this is not possible, and you're prepared to carry out renovations, check the location of the rooms: is it possible to change or add on to expose living rooms, to make living rooms face the right way, or to install skylights or clerestories?

Building a new home presents a different situation. Plan it with the living, dining, kitchen and family rooms facing north (south in the northern hemisphere). Rooms facing the other way can still receive winter warmth from the sun by designing the roof to include a clerestory. An attached greenhouse will direct the warmth of the sun into your house in winter, and in summer draw cool air through it.

(NB north and south are reversed in northern hemisphere.)

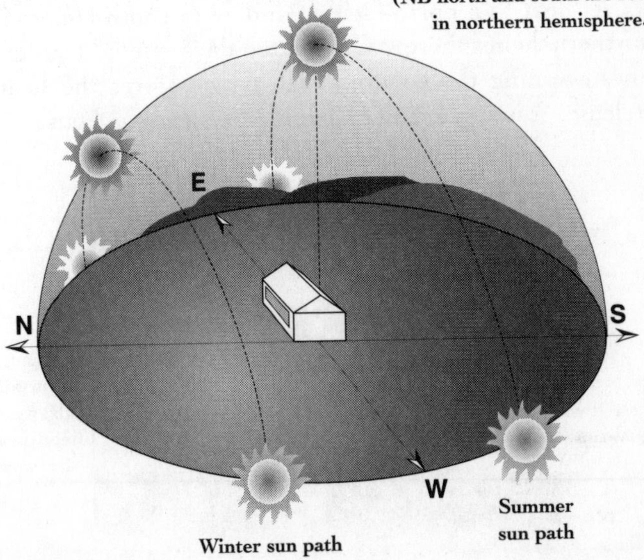

E

N

S

W

Winter sun path

Summer sun path

For maximum solar benefit the orientation of your house should be 10 degrees east of true north (10 degrees east of true south in the northern hemisphere). Where possible avoid installing windows on the east or west aspects, since they can cause your house to overheat in summer; north- and south-facing windows are best. Even when renovating you can plan your window arrangement, the ideal size being about 15 per cent of the floor area of the rooms, with living rooms up to a maximum of 20 per cent. Too much glass lets winter heat out and summer heat in by conduction ten times faster than an insulated wall.

The two key elements in passive-solar house design are glass and thermal mass. Glass is by far the simplest solar collector, in that it allows sunlight to enter the house, resulting in direct solar heat gain. Once the heat has entered the house through glazed areas, thermal mass comes into play. Basically, any part of your house that has the ability to store heat and release it later can be considered as thermal mass. Materials such as rock, concrete and brick have good thermal storage properties, so in most homes it will be masonry and brick walls and concrete slabs that make up the building's thermal mass.

One example of thermal mass at work is a concrete slab inside the house, next to a north-facing window (a south-facing one in the northern hemisphere). On winter days sunlight enters the window, warming the concrete slab which stores the heat and then releases it in the evening, helping to warm the house.

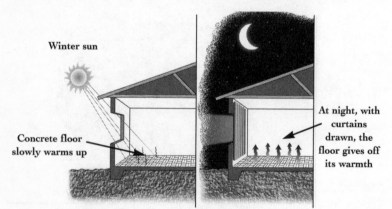

Winter sun

Concrete floor
slowly warms up

At night, with
curtains
drawn, the
floor gives off
its warmth

Thermal mass at work

A variety of successful and economical passive-solar methods for heating and cooling the house are discussed in Chapters 2 and 3.

PROTECTING YOUR HOUSE
FROM THE ELEMENTS

The success of any solar heating or cooling mechanisms you add to your house will depend upon how well the house is insulated from both the cold and the heat. And even if you don't make any solar modifications to your heating and cooling systems, by taking basic steps to insulate it properly you will cut down the amount of electricity you use running heaters, air conditioners and fans.

ALL ABOUT GLASS

Every area of plain window and door glass in your home is useful when you want to gain the heat of the sun because it allows about 80 per cent of the sun's radiant heat to pass through, as long as the sun is shining. This is great in on a winter's day but can be a disaster for your energy bills when the outdoor temperature differs sharply from the one you want indoors. This is because you can gain or lose as much as 12 times the amount of heat per square centimetre ($\frac{1}{6}$ square inch) of bare glass as you would through a completely uninsulated wall. Therefore it is important to ensure that household glazing works for you and not against you!

Window orientation, seasonal temperature extremes, and the wind can all contribute to how and when you should shade or insulate a window. Efficient window shading and the use of insulated drapes and blinds, and other options to exclude summer heat and retain winter warmth are discussed in detail in Chapters 2 and 3.

Types of glass

Glass comes in many different varieties which vary considerably in their reflecting and insulating qualities. Knowing what these variables are may have an effect on how you cover your window glass, or, in some circumstances, may even lead to its replacement.

Float glass

This is the name given to common window glass; it transmits about 80 per cent of all radiant heat from the sun.

Plate glass

It is about twice the thickness of common glass, but as far as energy efficiency is concerned differs very little.

Tempered glass

Though it is stronger than float and plate glass, and hence much safer, its thermal resistance is about the same.

Heat-absorbing glass

This type of glass usually comes in three different colours — gray, bronze or green, with a varying degree of opaqueness — and absorbs solar heat, and then reradiates it to both sides. It is best suited to cold-winter/cool-summer climates.

Reflective glass

Most people will recognise this glass by its mirror-like surface. A coating of transparent metallic oxide is fired onto the surface of plate glass so that it will reflect up to 70 per cent of solar heat gain as well as reducing light transmission by as much as 50 per cent.

Insulating glass

This is actually two pieces of float or plate glass separated by an insulating air space. If it is clear, it allows the same radiant heat gain as a single-glazed window, but has increased insulation value when the air space is 25 millimetres (1 inch) or more. Triple-glazing increases the thermal resistance even further, but its high cost may make it unviable.

Patterned glass

Patterned glass, which is usually installed in bathroom windows, can reduce solar heat gain to some degree, though it is nowhere near as effective as reflective or insulating glass.

FINDING YOUR HEAT LOSS

Quite often the most difficult thing to do when improving your home so that it is energy-efficient is to determine how effective your heating system is. Neither passive nor active systems will provide maximum output for minimum cost if cold air is finding its way in and warm air is escaping.

Wherever there's a way for cold air to get in where it's warm, it will. Leaks generally occur around and under doors, window sashes and panes, floorboards and under badly fitted skirting boards, as well as through power points. Even the pressure of wind exerted on a house can significantly increase the volume of cold air entering.

Methodically go through each room of your house and try to determine those areas where cold air is infiltrating. A lighted candle is a good indicator as to which direction draughts are coming from. As you pinpoint problems write them down, along with what you think the reasons are. Some of them may only require a simple remedy, while others may require some modifications, such as insulation, and you may therefore need the services of a professional contractor.

You will also need to check the heat distribution of your heating appliances. Quite often some rooms are left cold because bad design means that warm air is not being effectively distributed around the house. This type of problem can be easily solved by placing small vent openings in walls, and in two-storey homes in the floor, to redistribute warm air (see Chapter 2).

Another area of heat loss is through natural convection, and this is usually the greatest through the ceiling. It works like this: your heater warms the surrounding air, which expands, becomes less dense and rises, and is replaced by cooler, denser air. This is why you can still feel cold around the legs and feet. This problem can be remedied by installing ceiling fans to pull the warmer air down from the ceiling and redistribute it back down to lower levels. Most modern ceiling fans have a two-way switch so that their circulating cycle can be reversed for winter use.

Remember, thoroughness is the key when you check your home out for its heat losses. If you can diligently track down all the problem areas you'll be off to a good start.

Once you have found those areas where cold air is infiltrating you will need to take remedial steps to prevent it from entering your home.

Install draught excluders at the base of doors and foam insulating tape around door jambs. Windows should have effective storm mouldings, panes must be sealed tight with putty, and window frames caulked on the inside of the house. If you caulk them on the outside you'll have condensation problems.

If you can afford the cost, double glazing is very successful in preventing heat loss and cold-air penetration. Insulated curtains, which have a specially treated backing material, and close-fitting box pelmets, using the same material, will keep winter warmth from escaping and summer heat from entering. Where possible, make the curtains floor length. Tight-fitting blinds behind the curtains will also help.

Don't open windows unless it's absolutely necessary because when it's cold outside, heat escapes rapidly through open windows. In an average-sized room, with all windows and doors shut, there is one complete change of air each hour just through cracks around windows and doors.

If you feel that you must open a bedroom window at night during winter, then shut the bedroom door, and weatherstrip it to prevent heat from the rest of the house from being drawn under the door and lost out the window.

Skirting boards should be removed and refitted, or gaps filled. Usually, carpets with a thick underlay will solve this problem, as well as leaks through baseboards.

WRAPPING YOUR HOME
IN A THERMAL BLANKET

With cold-air infiltration problems solved it's now time to blanket your house with insulation, which will make both your heating and cooling systems more effective. If we all adequately insulated our homes it would greatly reduce our dependency on the use of non-renewable fuels to produce power for cooling and heating and thus help to eliminate much of the warming and pollution of our atmosphere.

When insulating, consider environmentally friendly alternatives in your choice of materials. Cellulose fibre is a natural, safe alternative made from recycled newspapers. It is one of the highest-rated insulating materials now available, cutting heating and cooling costs by up to 50 per cent. And not only is the fibre resistant to mice, rats, mildew, rot and fire, but it contains no asbestos or glass and is non-allergenic to human skin.

Other natural choices that are available for insulation include: wool, strawboard, sawdust, cork, vermiculite, pearlite, eel grass and treated seaweed. The downside of using these products is that they are susceptible to damp and vermin.

The best alternative to cellulose is rock wool, one of the most common home insulators next to fibreglass batts. It is spun from slag rock, then formed into blankets and batts, or shredded for hand-pouring in the ceiling or blowing into wall cavities. And because it is an inorganic material it has the added advantage that it will not burn. However, in many cases the wool blankets and batts have a vapour barrier bonded to them which is inflammable. It is preferable to use the shredded material and, where required, use a non-flammable vapour barrier.

In extremely hot climates window shutters can be used effectively, in conjunction with a thermal blanket, to keep the house cool. They can be adjusted to prevent the harsh hot summer sun from entering, while at the same time allowing a soft light and cooling breezes to penetrate.

It is also essential when insulating your home that you take into account large glass areas, such as picture windows on west-facing walls. During summer, the afternoon sun coming through the glass may well be trapped under the ceiling. This will make your home hotter during the night than it was before it was insulated. The answer is to provide adequate shading for the windows to prevent sun penetration and a summer heat problem.

Where to insulate

Insulation should not only be installed in the roof, but where possible in external wall cavities and under floorboards. You are then literally wrapping your house in a thermal blanket. However, wall insulation can usually only be fitted when building a new home or carrying out renovations. In some circumstances it is possible to accomplish cavity-wall insulation on existing homes by drilling holes and blowing the insulation into the wall. This choice should only be considered where environmentally friendly materials can be used. If you have a fibrocement or timber house, you could consider some form of cladding incorporating a layer of insulation. Deciduous creepers also help to reduce heat loss and won't affect mortar on brick homes. The leaves hold a thin layer of air against the walls and reduce the rate at which the wind carries heat away from the house. (If you consider deciduous vines a viable alternative, make sure you trim them each year. They can cause trouble in the eaves and in the roof.)

Floor insulation on existing homes does not pose the same problem as cavity-wall insulation: the material can be installed beneath floorboards and held in place between bearers by rodent-proof wire netting.

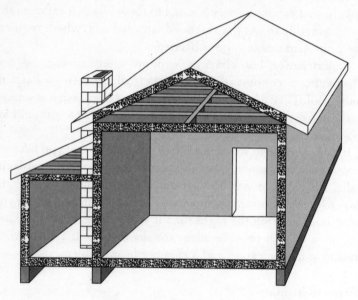

House wrapped in thermal blanket

Vapour barriers

An important factor to consider when wrapping your house in a thermal blanket is the inclusion of a vapour barrier to avoid moisture damage. Loose insulation that has been blown into wall cavities doesn't usually pose a moisture problem. However, if you think moisture is going to affect wall insulation, paint interior walls with a vapour-barrier paint. For roof insulation, consult a contractor or the insulation supplier about adding a vapour barrier

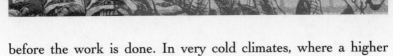

before the work is done. In very cold climates, where a higher number of layers of insulation need to be added, a vapour barrier is crucial. As warm air escapes from your home it carries moisture with it, and in cold climates and during winter this moisture can accumulate in the insulating material and ruin it. Everyday activities such as cooking, showering, washing and using a clothes dryer can add an enormous amount of moisture to the air.

Another problem associated with insulating is that moisture may collect on the inside of cold exterior wall surfaces and soak in, causing external paint to blister. In extreme circumstances it can accumulate sufficiently to stain interior walls and cause rot in timber framing. And the overall effectiveness of the insulation will be reduced wherever moisture accumulates.

Adequate roof ventilation is another significant consideration in preventing moisture build-up (see *Roof venting*, pages 64–67). A properly ventilated house will eliminate a substantial amount of moisture build-up. While vapour barriers are not a substitute for good ventilation, they will protect the insulation and ensure its effectiveness.

Vapour barriers are usually placed facing those surfaces that are warmest in winter. In the roof, insulation between the ceiling joists should have a vapour barrier between it and the ceiling lining, facing toward the rooms below. Vapour barriers should face inwards when used in exterior walls, upwards when used in under-floor insulation, and downwards when used with under-roof insulation (such as cathedral ceilings).

In extremely cold and damp climates, outside air may contain more moisture than that inside the house. If you live in this type of climate a vapour barrier may need to be placed toward the dampest (outside) air rather than the warmest. Before installation begins, however, it may be wise to first consult your insulation material supplier.

Other insulating options

When insulating external walls is impractical, covering interior surfaces can help to reduce heat loss in winter and energy usage. South-facing walls (north-facing ones in the northern hemisphere) that feel chilly on cold days are candidates for covering.

Covering the walls can be as simple as using a wall-hanging rug or panelling the wall with a more substantial covering. Wall hangings should cover as much of the wall as possible and for maximum insulating properties they should be made of wool rather than synthetics, and shag pile instead of smooth. Rough textures such as shag will keep air stiller along the wall, and air contributes to the insulation. A wall hanging that lends itself to being stretched over a timber frame and attached to the wall will be even more effective. The frame must have a continuous edge that is flush with the wall, and should have an air space behind it of at least 25 millimetres (1 inch). Although the air space is not essential, it will add considerably to the insulating properties.

Panelling over an existing wall will not only improve its insulating properties but will also allow you some degree of freedom with decoration. One of the most practical choices is to use a combination of 10 millimetre- ($\frac{2}{5}$ inch-) thick hardboard and 15 millimetre- ($\frac{3}{5}$ inch-) thick cork tiles. This is ideal for a south-facing bedroom (north-facing in the northern hemisphere), as it will not only insulate and provide a snug room but the wall can also be used for displaying posters, drawings, etc.

To fit your insulating panel wall first attach the hardboard directly on top of the existing wall surface to the wall studs, using screws. All joins should be filled with a suitable caulking compound before gluing the cork in place. Choose the largest cork tiles that you can purchase — 60 x 100 centimetres ($23\frac{1}{2}$ x 39 inches) is an ideal size — and glue in place with a good glue, preferably an acoustical adhesive. To prevent a line-up of the vertical joints commence every other row with a tile cut in half.

If using panelling on an interior masonry wall you will first need to fix horizontal battens, placed at 60 centimetre ($23\frac{1}{2}$ inch) intervals. Suitable timber for battens is 25 x 50 millimetre (1 x 2 inch) radiata pine, which can be attached to the masonry wall with an appropriate glue, such as liquid nails, or by drilling the wall at 60 centimetre ($23\frac{1}{2}$ inch) intervals along the line of each batten, inserting a screwing-plug, and then screwing each batten in place. The creation of an air space between the wall and hardboard by the battens will add to the overall insulating properties.

Insulating concrete slabs

This would seem to be a somewhat bizarre project, since efforts to insulate under an existing slab would not only be impractical but highly expensive. However, simple modifications will help to eliminate the need to live with cold floors by reducing the amount of cold that can seep in from the outside.

The foundation around the slab's perimeter can be protected with rigid panels of polyurethane or polystyrene. Dig a narrow trench about 60 centimetres (23½ inches) deep and brush all the dirt off the foundation with a wire brush. Install a metal drip cap around the perimeter, forcing it if possible under weatherboards or other siding. Nail into position and caulk the top edge with a silicone sealant.

On masonry wall construction it may be necessary to remove some of the mortar between one of the lower courses to form a continuous groove in which to fit the drip cap. Repoint the groove with mortar to form a weatherproof bond and to hold the drip cap in place.

Coat the rigid insulating material with a mastic adhesive and press into position under the drip cap and against the side of the foundation to form a firm bond. To avoid any possible weather damage coat the top third of the insulation with cement, allow to dry, then replace the dirt.

IN PURSUIT OF A 'ZERO DISCHARGE HOUSEHOLD'

By ensuring that your house is well insulated you'll be conserving electricity already. If you then solarise your home you can successfully tap into the sun's energy, and use this free energy to reduce, or completely eliminate, the need to use fossil fuel-based energy systems. By effectively implementing the improvements already discussed, and making other energy conservation improvements as discussed in the following chapters, you will be well on the way to turning your home into a 'zero discharge household' which minimises energy wastage while maintaining a comfortable household climate.

The optimum level of energy conservation is obviously going to vary from home to home, and in many cases will be dependent upon readily available finances and the balance between initial costs and energy saved. However, many of the changes can be carried out inexpensively, often by yourself. For the handyperson it may be something as simple as building your own passive-solar hot water system, or adding an attached greenhouse to capture the sun's rays for winter warmth or summer cooling. Whatever your improvements, they will contribute to turning your home into a paragon of energy efficiency.

ENERGY-EFFICIENT HEADING

Space heating with solar energy is by far the most cost effective way of tapping the sun's energy. Drawing back the curtains on a north-facing wall (south-facing in the northern hemisphere) and letting sunlight in through the windows is the simplest way to heat your house. The entering sunlight is absorbed by the furnishings in the room and released as heat. However, unless your windows are covered at night with some form of insulating material, such as curtains with an insulated lining, more heat may be lost at night than was gained during the day.

However, if you want to substantially heat your home this way, windows would need to cover a large part of the north wall (or the south wall in the northern hemisphere). Even then, solar heat gain would be limited on cloudy days and could well be nil during rainy weather.

The answer is a combination of both passive-solar and active systems, including the addition of more effective solar-heating systems. Active systems that use very little fossil fuel energy or a renewable energy source, such as low-cost heat pumps or slow combustion wood heaters, are ideal.

In this chapter I will give you a number of simple alternatives to get as much of the sun's energy as possible into your home for winter warmth, and also show you how to effectively store the heat and distribute it through the house at night.

MINIMISE HEATING

Sadly, most homes rely on inefficient and expensive heating systems to keep us warm. Electric heaters, or reverse cycle air conditioners, pump out kilowatts of wasted energy in a vain attempt to heat every room in the house, which of course is totally unnecessary.

Even if it is not financially possible for you to implement solar heating systems in your house, you will find that your heating bills will be much lower if you only heat the areas of the house that you most occupy. In open-plan houses, where living areas are all open and interconnected, you will need to heat the whole house in winter. If the house has a cathedral ceiling, remember that the expensive hot air will end up just under the ceiling. Try to close off the room that you spend most time in from the rest of the house and install a low amperage, or solar/battery powered, reverse cycle ceiling fan to force hot air back down around your feet. Reverse cycle ceiling fans are also effective in reducing fuel consumption when used in conjunction with a slow-combustion wood heater.

DRESS NATURALLY TO SAVE ENERGY

A practical, non-polluting way of reducing energy wastage in winter, that's simple and effective, is to take advantage of your body's own heat engine. Your body's natural warmth is just like a heating element that can be put to good use to provide a comfortable environment, provided that the heat is not allowed to radiate away. Put on a jumper or other clothes, or more blankets on the bed, rather than switching on the heater or an electric blanket. You will soon adapt to the cooler temperature inside your home, and you won't feel as great a shock when you venture out.

The Chinese are well aware of this principle and wear energy-saving layers of clothing to stay warm in winter. There's never been enough fuel to squander in China, so people have learnt to get along extremely well in cooler homes and public buildings by dressing in energy-efficient clothing. They wear cotton underwear, woollen over-clothing on their upper and lower bodies, and then a heavy cotton suit. Although they may not be dressed for style, they are certainly dressed for warmth and comfort.

The most efficient, lightweight insulating garments we can wear are ones made from natural materials such as wool and cotton. Padded jackets and quilts insulate your body from feeling the cold by trapping a layer of air between the fabric and your skin. Your body's 'heat engine' then takes over. The most effective of all natural materials is goose down. Because it 'breathes', when it is sewn between layers of fabric in clothing or bedding, it transfers body moisture to the outside of the fabric, where it evaporates. A down quilt on your bed will not only keep you comfortably warm in the most frigid of conditions, but will ensure that there's no energy drain or increase in your electricity bill.

A woollen cap is also a must both indoors and outdoors in cold weather. If your head is cold, your feet, hands and the rest of your body will also be cold. Blood is pumped up to warm the head at the expense of reduced flow — and reduced warmth — to other parts of the body.

GETTING THE SUN INSIDE

Without exception, the primary goal of any solar heating modification is to get as much sun inside your home as possible. Whatever solar modifications you make to your home, their effectiveness will depend primarily upon the use of glazing, be it glass or plastic. The ways of handling solar heat gain are only outnumbered by the many different ways glazing can be used to get the sun inside your home. The following simple, passive systems will bring both heat and day-lighting into your living space, and at the same time add value to your property.

SKYLIGHTS

A well placed skylight can transform an otherwise dark recess of a room into a bright, sunny living area. Not only will you get a view of the sky, your indoor plants will get a new lease on life. Even a modest skylight measuring 60 square centimetres (10 square inches) will, on a cloudy day, flood the room below it with natural light equivalent to three 100 watt light bulbs. If it faces north (or south in the northern hemisphere), it will also contribute to direct-gain heat, and if fitted with a closeable vent, will allow hot air to escape in summer.

There are a number of commercially manufactured skylight units available that can be installed quite easily by the home handyperson. If installed in a location that isn't too shaded during winter, skylights can be placed up to 420 centimetres (165 inches) from the floor, without too much loss of light.

The amount of light gain from the skylight is dependent upon its size and orientation. A good rule of thumb is that the skylight should be the size of approximately 5 per cent of the floor area to be illuminated. If the room is extremely large, it may be better to have two or three smaller skylights rather than one gigantic one — this will also give you more even light distribution.

You may wish to have insulated louvres fitted to the skylight to prevent heat from escaping or entering on cold winter nights or hot summer days.

Building your own skylight louvres

Measure your skylight opening and make a butt-jointed frame from 50 x 25 millimetre (2 x 1 inch) dressed timber that will fit inside it. Divide its length evenly to find out how many louvres you need and what their outside dimension should be. Each louvre should be around 1600 millimetres (63 inches) wide.

Next construct the required number of louvre frames from dressed timber 25 x 13 millimetres (1 x ½ inch), making them a little shorter than the width of the skylight frame. Glue and tack 3 millimetre (¹⁄₁₀ inch) hardboard on one side, fill the frame with natural cellulose fibre insulation, and fix 3 millimetre (¹⁄₁₀ inch) hardboard on the remaining side, allowing one of the hardboard sides to extend 10 millimetres (²⁄₅ inch) below the frame (this overlap helps to seal the louvres so that warm air won't escape).

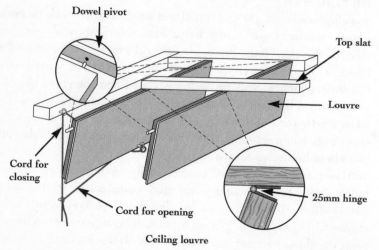

Dowel pivot

Top slat

Louvre

Cord for closing

Cord for opening

25mm hinge

Ceiling louvre

Hinge the centre top of each louvre to a 50 x 25 millimetre (2 x 1 inch) slat; fit them into the frame and drill 12 millimetre- ($\frac{1}{2}$ inch-) holes through the frame and into the centre of each louvre end and then secure with 40 millimetre- ($1\frac{1}{2}$ inch-) long dowel pivots. Nail the unit into place.

Insert close-eyed screws into the centre of the bottom frame and bottom louvre, and into the wall just below the frame eye. Thread a cord up through the wall eye and frame eye, then through the louvre eye and back down through the wall eye. Tie the cord ends to a metal cleat screwed to the wall.

CLERESTORIES

Clerestories are in effect large skylights which, instead of being installed flush to the roof, are set at an angle. They allow far more solar gain than a skylight. Their vertical, or slightly tilted, glazing also gives you far more control over when and where sunlight will enter. The result is direct-gain space heating and daytime lighting on a scale you never imagined possible.

To provide shade from unwanted summer heat gain your clerestory should include a roof overhang — this will still allow the low winter sun to penetrate. To reduce heat loss in winter, heavy curtains with a lining of suitable insulating material need to be hung from closed pelmets attached to a sill board so that warm air doesn't rise between the curtain and the glass.

Unless you are building a new home, a clerestory will mean major structural changes to your roof: rafters, ceiling joists and other structural components. Not all existing houses may be able to accommodate such an alteration; cost or complexity may make the project unfeasible, but it is worth careful consideration.

Factors to consider before embarking on such a project are: on a steeply pitched roof it may not be possible to locate a clerestory close enough to living rooms to warm them effectively. A steep pitch would more than likely require an unattractive amount of vertical glass that may detract from the overall appearance of your house. Shallow-pitched roofs are more suited to this type of solar-gain heating system. For the clerestory to work effectively, the ridge of the roof needs to run as close as possible to the east-west axis, or at least within 30 degrees of it. If your house has a flat roof, a clerestory can be orientated to receive maximum sunlight and heat gain no matter which way the house faces.

As with all solar collectors, shading is an important factor to consider if you intend to build a clerestory. A clerestory will not work effectively if shaded by trees or buildings in winter, however shading is not likely to be a major problem because of the clerestory's location on the roof.

Because this type of construction requires a structural alteration to your house your local council or planning body will require the lodgment of building plans. Unless you are reasonably proficient in building construction, a qualified tradesperson should be engaged to carry out the alterations. It would also be wise to seek professional design advice before you start, otherwise the finished project may not measure up to your expectations.

THE SUNROOM

A glassed-in room, porch or verandah is a simple passive-solar system which has tremendous potential. It should face the north (south in the northern hemisphere) and should be attached to a room that needs daytime heating, such as the kitchen, family room or lounge.

On the wall between the sunroom and the other rooms of the house, ventilators should be fitted both close to the floor and close to the ceiling. These ventilators should be fitted with shutters which can be closed at night, or partially closed when the sunroom is being used for summer cooling. In addition to these ventilators, there should also be adjustable roof venting.

During summer, the top wall ventilator should be closed and the roof vents opened. As the air in the sunroom heats up, it will be convected through the roof vents and replaced by cooler air from inside the house. By opening south-facing windows or ventilators (north-facing ones in the northern hemisphere), cool air will be continually drawn through the house, maintaining a comfortable temperature.

During winter, the roof vents should be closed, both the top and bottom inside ventilators opened, and south-facing (north-facing in the northern hemisphere) windows or ventilators closed. Again, the same principle applies: cooler air is drawn from the house, is heated, and instead of being discharged into the atmosphere, is redirected into the house. Small, low-amperage or solar-powered fans can be fitted in the top ventilators to make them more effective.

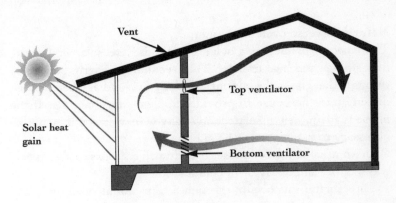

Winter warming (roof vent closed)

ATTACHED GREENHOUSE

If you have room for one, a greenhouse attached to the side of your house will provide winter warmth, summer cooling, added living space and somewhere to grow out-of-season vegetables if you're a keen gardener. It can also serve as a useful winter entrance hall, acting as an air-lock heat trap and reducing the likelihood of cold air entering the house with visitors.

Basically, all greenhouses are solar, but an attached greenhouse differs from a traditional free-standing one in that it incorporates additional mass for heat storage and is attached to a north-facing wall of the house (a south-facing one in the northern hemisphere) so that as well as providing good conditions for growing plants and a possible winter garden retreat, it also warms the house in winter and cools it in summer, thus reducing energy consumption.

Add a verandah or shade house on the opposite side of the house to increase the effectiveness of your greenhouse or sunroom for summer cooling. Open adjacent windows or doors during the day; as the air in the greenhouse heats up and is discharged, cool air will be drawn in from outside through doors and windows on the opposite side of the house and circulated through it. At night, simply close off the greenhouse ventilators till the air warms up from the next day's sunlight.

A greenhouse need not be an expensive, permanent structure. Prefabricated kits, where glass panels simply slot into a framework, are readily available.

Nature's reverse cycle heat pump

The basic principles of a solar greenhouse are solar collection, heat storage and heat transfer. The greenhouse absorbs solar heat through the glass, the air inside heats up, and is then vented directly into the house to provide supplementary heating. If the house is adequately insulated, on sunny winter days it may not be necessary to use any other form of heating.

In an attached greenhouse, heat transfer occurs in four basic ways, either singularly or in combination.

1. Direct gain: this occurs through a transparent opening in the common wall between the greenhouse and residence.
2. Direct air exchange: this occurs between the greenhouse and residence via lower and upper vents in the wall or through doors and windows.
3. Conduction: if the common wall is an uninsulated masonry or frame wall, heat can be transferred through the wall itself.
4. Remote storage: heat can be transferred to a thermal mass storage area, such as a hollow-core masonry wall filled with rocks, and used later to heat the house.

A greenhouse should include a facility for the exchange of hot air, since neither direct gain heat nor conduction are likely to be adequate for the transfer of heat into the residence. Although openings such as windows and doors in the common wall will allow the adequate natural transfer of heat (convection), forced convection will ensure that the residence does not overheat, a likely risk if the solar greenhouse incorporates thermal mass. Forced convection will also ensure that the greenhouse operates at maximum efficiency as a reverse cycle pump during summer to cool your home.

The principle of forced convection is simple, and requires only the installation of shuttered upper and lower vents in the common wall. The upper vent incorporates a low-amperage or solar-powered fan to boost air flow from the greenhouse to the residence in winter.

In summer, the upper vent is kept closed and the hot air is discharged to the atmosphere through vents in the greenhouse roof. Adjoining windows and doors are protected with insulated blinds or curtains to prevent radiated or convected heat penetrating the living space.

During winter, the greenhouse roof vents are kept closed, and the upper common wall vent is opened during the daytime for heating but closed at night so that heat inside the house doesn't escape. A one-way flap should be installed on the lower vent to prevent the cycle from reversing itself at night and replacing warmed interior air with cold air. Curtains or blinds should also be drawn at night on windows or doors adjoining the greenhouse to minimise heat loss.

Because a solar greenhouse stores and transfers heat that is collected during the day it creates an energy system. This collected heat is stored in a thermal mass. Depending upon your thermal mass set-up, at night stored heat will then be radiated back into the greenhouse or into the residence when outside temperatures become cooler than the stored mass.

Building your solar greenhouse

The creation of a convection loop — the movement of warm air between the greenhouse and the inside of your house — is essential for the greenhouse to heat or cool your house. For this reason it is best built in front of one or two windows and a door. This will not only facilitate access between the house and the greenhouse, but will cut down on the expense of major structural work on the outside wall of the house to provide a convection loop.

For your solar greenhouse to function successfully it should be attached to a wall that faces within 30 degrees east or west of true north (true south in the northern hemisphere), and that is structurally capable of becoming the thermal mass wall of the greenhouse. Examine the house's structure at possible attachment points to make sure that the masonry, studs, beams or joists are strong enough to support the added load of the greenhouse. It is very important when siting it that nothing will block the sunlight, especially when the sun dips to its lowest winter path.

The key to successfully designing a solar greenhouse is first deciding what you really want out of it. For instance, there is no sense in constructing it primarily as a food production centre if it will remain fallow for most of the year. Ideally, it should be a combination of passive heat collector, relaxing sun space, and food-production or ornamental plant-growing space.

You will also need to give careful consideration to exactly how much of a north-facing wall (south-facing in the northern hemisphere) you wish to devote to your greenhouse, and whether you want glazing only on the roof and front, or if your budget allows for side-wall glazing as well. When you've thought about it and sketched until you cannot possibly squeeze another centimetre of glazed area into your plans, you're ready to start building. But don't forget, before you rush off to buy, salvage or beg the building materials, the plans will have to be submitted to your local council or planning body.

Foundation and floor

Proper support for your greenhouse is essential and will be required by your local council or planning body. In most circumstances a poured concrete footing around the perimeter of the greenhouse, including a 12 millimetre ($\frac{1}{2}$ inch) reinforcing bar, is all that's needed. This should be topped with a single course of concrete blocks, to which the bottom plate of your greenhouse framing can be attached.

It is essential that you provide adequate exterior insulation around the footing. Rigid 25 millimetre (1 inch) polystyrene sheeting, or other material recommended in your local building code, should be placed against the exterior foundation, extending at least 60 centimetres ($23\frac{1}{2}$ inches) below ground level, or in very cold areas below the frost line. This will prevent heat escaping from the greenhouse and being lost into the ground outside.

The floor of the greenhouse should be left uncovered if you intend to propagate plants. Once your garden beds have been established you can then lay pavers in the areas in between. If you intend to use the structure purely as a heat pump, you should cover the floor of the greenhouse with concrete, brick, sandstone flagging, pavers, or any similar material that will contribute mass for heat storage. For maximum efficiency, the floor can be underlaid with insulating plastic or other insulating material to reduce heat loss to the ground.

External walls

The north-facing wall (south-facing in the northern hemisphere) is the primary source of solar radiation, and if finances permit should be double glazed. However, you can use high-quality clear fibreglass, plexiglass or polyethylene and still have an effective greenhouse.

In traditional attached greenhouse design, the north wall (the south wall in the northern hemisphere), leans outward at an angle of 60 degrees, for maximum exposure to winter sun. However, in climates with mild winters and very hot summers it is more advantageous to build a vertical wall. Although a vertical wall will reduce the heat absorbed during the winter months by about 25 per cent, it carries the benefit of halving heat gain in summer.

East and west walls need not always be glazed, provided they are solid, well insulated and caulked to prevent heat and cold from entering or escaping.

Thermal mass wall

Depending on what you intend your greenhouse to do, thermal mass for heat storage may be unnecessary. During winter, only one-third of an average household's heating consumption occurs during daylight hours, so if your greenhouse is primarily a passive heating system, the house should absorb most of the heat from the greenhouse without it overheating. This essentially avoids the need for thermal storage.

However, sometimes it is necessary to store heat to prevent overheating, minimise day–night temperature changes and provide comfortable temperatures when the greenhouse forms part of the night-time living area.

If horticultural activities will be an important part of your greenhouse's function, then thermal mass is essential because the temperature in the greenhouse will fluctuate less dramatically. The greater the amount of mass, the smaller the temperature fluctuations.

The most important thermal mass in the greenhouse is its southern wall (northern in the northern hemisphere), which it shares with the house. Unless the existing common wall is made of masonry, the cost of constructing a thermal storage wall will add considerably to the overall construction costs. Placing a number of 200 litre (44 gallon) drums filled with water in front of the existing wall is an easier and less expensive means of achieving the same result. They can be stacked three high, providing a strong, rigid board is placed between the layers. They should be sealed and painted with a matt black paint to increase heat absorption. To inhibit corrosion of the drums, each 200 litres (44 gallons) of water should be treated with ¼ cup (60 mL/ 2 fl oz) of sodium dichromate. Make sure not to plant any leafy, tall plants in a position where they will cast shadows on the drums. You will need approximately 60 cubic centimetres (3½ cubic inches) of water for every 30 square centimetres (4½ square inches) of glazing. On the other hand, if you build a masonry wall, you will need 34 kilograms (75 pounds) of masonry (rock) for every 30 square centimetres (4½ square inches), five times the weight of the water required. For this reason, if you don't have a pre-existing masonry wall, water-filled drums are a desirable option.

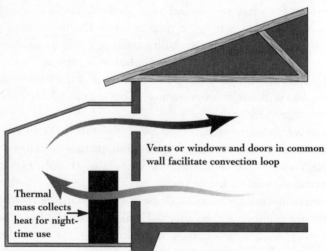

Vents or windows and doors in common wall facilitate convection loop

Thermal mass collects heat for night-time use

Thermal mass in the greenhouse

Another alternative to building a solid masonry wall is to construct a thermal mass unit next to the external house wall, using the same amount of rock contained in wire mesh. It must be well ventilated so that air can circulate between the rocks in order to carry heat.

A word of caution: be careful not to overdo thermal storage. Stay within the guidelines mentioned above, as an excess of thermal mass will warm up too slowly, reducing the amount of heat available to the house.

For those of you who endeavour to maintain a self-sufficient or self-reliant type of lifestyle, you can take heat storage one step further. Consider installing a concrete water tank in the greenhouse as a thermal mass. Not only will it absorb heat, but it can also be used to grow and farm tropical food fish.

Roof

If building a traditional greenhouse with a sloping north wall (or south wall in the northern hemisphere), the roof of the house can be extended or a regular roof built from the house to where it joins the greenhouse wall. A combination of half glazing and half standard roofing material may be a good choice if you intend to propagate plants all year round. Where the north wall (the south wall in the northern hemisphere) is vertical, the combination roof should be adopted to let in the maximum amount of winter sun. A screen can be installed to filter summer sun, or it can be shaded with a heavy material to exclude sunlight altogether.

Ventilation

During cooler weather the hot air that collects under the roof of the greenhouse is vented directly into the house for heating. Vents to encourage cooler air from the house to flow into the greenhouse for warming should be located near the floor. Roughly 30 square centimetres ($4\frac{1}{2}$ square inches) of this vent space is required for every 250–300 square centimetres of transparent surface material on the north-facing side (south-facing in the northern hemisphere).

Air can be permitted to circulate naturally by convection, or assisted with a low-amperage or solar-powered fan activated by a thermostat. Vents will also need to be provided in the roof to discharge hot air during the warmer months, which is essential if your greenhouse is to function as a solar air-conditioning unit as well. These outlet vents should be placed downwind to exhaust the hot air. If you have trouble overcoming the problem of rain leaking through the vents, it would be worth considering the installation of boat-hatch vents or the type commonly used in caravans.

Vents should also be included in the east and west walls to provide cross-ventilation. A vent should be installed near the floor of the side which is usually windward, and on the opposite side a vent should be located near the roof. You should provide about 30 square centimetres (4½ square inches) of side-wall vents for about every 500 centimetres (7¾ square inches) of floor space. All vents should be designed so that they will be airtight when closed.

Connecting vents between the greenhouse and residence may need to be closed at night during winter to prevent hot air escaping when the greenhouse temperature falls. During hot summer days they should also be kept closed, unless venting for solar air conditioning. Screening the common wall vents is also important to keep insects and other unwanted creatures from invading your living space. This will, however, require larger vents since insect screens impede the natural convection flow.

Weatherproofing
Once your greenhouse is erected and complete it is important to ensure that it will work as efficiently as possible. This means weatherstripping and caulking every external opening, crack or nail hole. Solid external walls should be well insulated and areas around windows, doors and vents sealed. To prevent plants from growing in the direction of their primary light source, the upper areas of the rear wall, the underside of the roof and timber framing should be painted bright white.

Choosing materials to control the sunlight
The intensity of sunlight entering a greenhouse not only has an important impact on its thermal performance but also on the growth of the plants inside. Since plants primarily use visible light

for growth, and prefer to receive it as diffused sunlight in varying amounts, it is important to use glazing materials that will provide those conditions for the plants and at the same time maximise the effectiveness of the greenhouse as a solar heat pump.

The use of materials such as fibreglass or reinforced plastic will aid in the diffusion of the entering sunlight. The scattering of the light by the glazing material can be further enhanced by painting all the interior surfaces, with the exception of the common thermal wall, thermal mass and glazing, with a matt white paint. It is not advisable to use tinted glazing materials or coloured paints as the plants may suffer stunted growth and you may have a poor yield of vegetables. Similarly, growing problems can also occur if glazing or paints absorb too much sunlight in the visible region. However, this should not be a problem if quality glazing materials, such as acrylics or polycarbonates, are used.

The continuing success of a productive solar greenhouse, for space heating and cooling and the growing of plants, is a balance between transmitted solar energy, temperature and moisture. Under optimum conditions, a well designed and built solar greenhouse is able to collect in the vicinity of three times the required solar energy needed for daytime space heating of the greenhouse and plant photosynthesis.

Though this excess heat can be used for heating your house in winter, daytime overheating can still occur, especially in summer. For this reason, steps must be taken to reduce the amount of solar radiation reaching the interior of the greenhouse. A sun screen, for instance, can be put in place during the hot summer months. However, you must be careful when choosing a sun screen as there are limits to the amount of solar radiation that can be reduced without negatively affecting horticultural production and thermal performance. If, for example, entering sunlight is reduced by more than 70 per cent, the remaining light is insufficient to support photosynthesis in crop plants, and very little energy is left for thermal storage. You must strike an environmental balance by filtering the sunlight with a suitable screening material, such as cheesecloth. The holes in cheesecloth transmit all light equally and the white cloth reflects and scatters the light back out of the greenhouse.

Plant propagation and food production

Food production in a solar greenhouse takes full advantage of all that available free sunlight which provides the optimum environment for plant growth. For those people who enjoy growing their own fresh vegetables all year round, initial greenhouse construction costs will quickly be offset against savings made at the local supermarket. This payback period will be even shorter when you take into consideration the saving on energy bills.

A solar greenhouse is an ecosystem in its own right and can operate as either an open or closed system. For growing vegetables and ornamental plants the open system (in which the windows and roof are left open to the elements) provides a far more natural environment, and will allow natural pollination of plants to occur. However, if you intend to use your greenhouse to propagate specialised plants, such as orchids, a closed system should be considered.

For information about preparing soil for use in the greenhouse, see Chapter 7.

Watering greenhouse plants

The amount of watering you need to do in the greenhouse will vary according to plant types and seasonal weather conditions. Overwatering can be just as disastrous as underwatering. Too much water eliminates air pockets in the soil and can promote disease and other disorders, while too little water will stress your plants and stunt their growth.

Establish a schedule for checking plant beds and only add water when required. A moisture-content test can be made by taking a pinch of soil from below the surface of your planting bed. If it's just wet enough to hold together without crumbling, it's usually moist enough to support mature plant growth.

Water temperature is also important; ideally it should be around 21 degrees Celsius (70 degrees Fahrenheit). Most tap water is considerably colder and will need to be warmed first. This can be done by first running the water through a black hose attached to the thermal wall or along the inside of the glass.

To improve the effectiveness of plant-watering you should consider a subsurface trickle irrigation system. Water is stored in a holding tank, which is painted black and placed where it will receive direct sunlight; this will raise the temperature of the water sufficiently. A gate valve is installed in the bottom of the tank, to which is attached a length of perforated garden hose. Multi-filament double-braided rope is threaded through the length of the hose (see *Low-cost drip-watering system*, page 138). The hose is then run beneath the surface of your garden beds, throughout the whole area. The beds can be watered by opening the gate valve just enough for the water to barely flow out. Provided the base of the holding tank is higher than ground level, water will gradually flow through the rope and trickle out the holes in the hose.

Pest control

The lush habitat of a solar greenhouse can become the home of many insects. However, not all the insects that thrive in its environment are pests; insects such as ladybugs and lacewings are beneficial predators that can help to keep unwanted pests in check. The key is to maintain a balance between the pests and the insects that are the natural enemies of the pests. If the greenhouse is allowed to overheat, beneficial insects such as ladybirds will vacate the greenhouse and the plants will transpire excessively. The result is weaker plants, inhibited pollination, reduced yields and a breeding ground for pests and diseases.

Because the greenhouse ecosystem is so different to that of the garden you will have to give nature a helping hand to establish an acceptable environment for your plants. The first step is to prevent overheating by regularly monitoring the greenhouse temperature and making use of adjustable external vents, which, in any event, should be fully open during the summer. Companion planting must be practised at all times, as it will restrict the mobility and breeding rate of the insect pest population (see *Companion planting*, pages 140–144).

Organic-based insecticides and fungicides with a short lifespan can be used to a limited degree, but only when absolutely necessary, and only when the daily activities of beneficial predator insects have ceased (see *Pest control without pesticides*, pages 145–152).

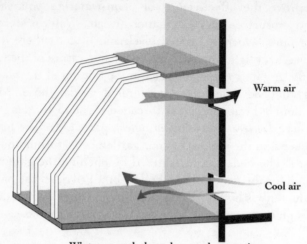

Winter warmth through natural convection

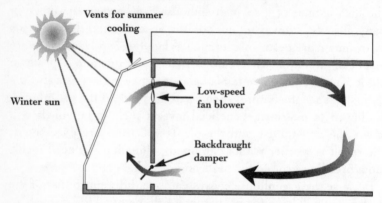

Vents open for winter warmth

WINDOW GREENHOUSE

A north-facing window (or a south-facing one in the northern hemisphere) can easily be turned into an effective greenhouse to make the most of the winter sun. As well as providing additional warmth, it can be used to grow herbs, flowers and even tomatoes all year round. Add adjustable shelves to provide extra space for all your potted plants, and a hanging rod at the top to dry clothing.

Your window greenhouse should extend approximately 60 centimetres (23½ inches) from the windowsill and can either be framed and glazed or made from an old window sash. If the unit fits under the eave, flashing may not be needed. Otherwise, use a suitable waterproof material, such as galvanised tin plate which is available from most hardware stores. Seal screws or holes with a waterproof sealant.

THERMAL MASS

HEAT STORAGE WALL

The heat storage wall consists of a wall built of double brick or concrete blocks that have had the hollow cores filled with concrete; the outside of the wall is painted black. A layer of glass is added onto the external wall, with an air space of 15–30 centimetres (6–12 inches) between the masonry and the glazing.

The air trapped in the space between the wall and the glass heats up, and heat is stored in the brick or concrete of the wall. Vents high in the wall and close to the ground allow the warm air, by natural convection, to circulate into the house during the day; the heat stored in the wall is released at night. A low-amperage or solar-powered fan can be installed in the upper vent for increased efficiency. A thermostat can be fitted to the fan so that it will automatically shut off when the collector is cold, so that it does not circulate cold air into the house.

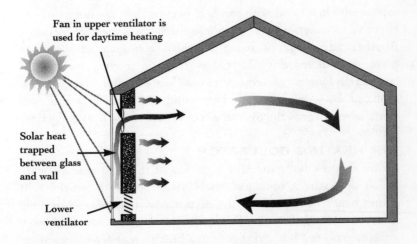

Fan in upper ventilator is used for daytime heating

Solar heat trapped between glass and wall

Lower ventilator

Heat storage wall

Shutters should be fitted to both top and bottom ventilators so that the unit can be shut off in summer; the bottom ventilator should also be fitted with a one-way flap to prevent the unit from reversing its cycle at night.

The glazing must be vented so that summer heat can escape; small awning-type windows that are lockable from the outside are ideal. To prevent air from escaping when the vents are closed, weather-proof stripping should be fitted around the inside of the frames of the glazing. If the framework fits snugly under the eave, and is protected from moisture and rainwater, flashing will not be required. Otherwise, install a suitable flashing along the top plate.

SUN TRAPS

Sun traps absorb the warmth of winter sun during the day and then radiate the heat at night when the house begins to cool off. Sun traps are simple to make: large dark-coloured pots, sand-filled tubs, or dark-coloured steel drums filled with water and sealed will suffice. Place these outside in the sun during the day then bring them inside at night — or place them inside the house in front of a sunny window.

The heat capacity of any portable thermal mass depends entirely on the material used. Masonry pots have a reasonably high heat capacity because of their density, which is further increased when filled with sand. However, they are not nearly as effective as water, which has two to three times the heat capacity. Another advantage of using a sealed container of water in preference to masonry is that water is a moving mass — a convection loop is created that causes heated water to rise and be replaced by cooler water. This continual mixing within the container improves the overall effectiveness of the heat collection.

AIR HEATING COLLECTOR

An air heating collector is a variation of the heat storage wall, which utilises roof solar absorbers. Absorber plates on the roof gather heat from the sun at the hottest part of the day. Warm air is forced around the collector during the day by a low-amperage or solar-powered fan and then into a heat storage tank, consisting of a hollow insulated wall filled with rocks which retain the heat.

At night the fan is switched off and a second fan delivers stored heat into the house as required.

The solar collectors are constructed as illustrated for the solar air-conditioning unit (see page 68). They should be divided into sections to suit the width of the absorber plate material. For maximum efficiency, the angle of each collector to the horizontal should be the angle of the latitude where you live plus 10 degrees. Absorber plates need to be quite large; in areas where frosts are common they should have a surface area of not less than 50 square metres (540 square feet).

For collector ducts, either use commercially manufactured ducting or make them from timber particle board, lined with an aluminium foil insulation such as roof sarking.

The masonry heat storage tank is to be filled with rocks of varying sizes, but no larger than 20 centimetres (7½ inches) in diameter. The tank must stand on a solid foundation, since the total finished weight will be several tonnes (tons).

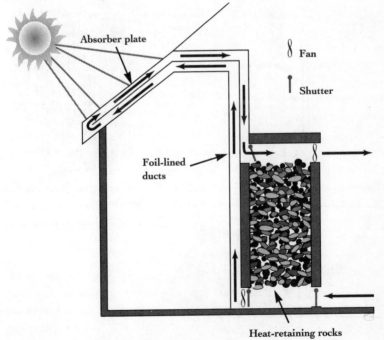

Roof hot air collector

EXTERNAL MODULAR WALL AIR HEATER

One of the simplest solar hot air collectors, the external modular wall air heater is a box made up of double-glazing on one side and a corrugated iron absorber panel (aluminium can be substituted for lightness) on the other side, backed with ridged insulation. The unit is mounted onto the external wall of the house. When the sun's rays strike the absorber panel, the air behind it is heated, which then rises and enters the house through a top vent. Cool air from inside the house is then drawn through a bottom vent, heated, and the cycle continues.

One wall air heater can be used on its own, or several can be placed along the wall for maximum effect, the width of each being about the distance between three framing studs and the length to match the height of the wall. They should always be located on a north-facing wall (south-facing in the northern hemisphere). The delivery of heated air can be assisted by a low-speed, low-amperage or solar-powered fan.

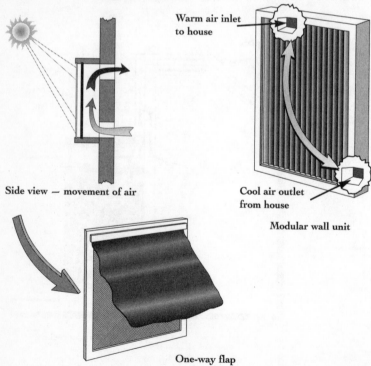

Side view — movement of air

Warm air inlet
to house

Cool air outlet
from house

Modular wall unit

One-way flap

The absorber plate must be corrugated to help to relieve the stresses of expansion and contraction, as well as to increase the heat-exchange area. Both sides of the absorber plate should be painted black for maximum heat absorption and radiation into the air channel. Proper surface preparation and priming are essential for good paint adhesion and long life.

The top of the collector box must be waterproofed with a suitable flashing and storm-moulding must be fitted around the entire perimeter between the frame and the wall. Use silicone sealant on any areas that present a leakage problem. The collector box must made as airtight as possible to keep the weather out and the hot air in. It is also important to have a reflective surface attached to the ridged insulation at the back of the unit to limit heat transfer into the wall of the house — use aluminium foil, with the shiny side facing into the collector box.

Fix shutters to both top and bottom vents and a one-way flap to the bottom vent, in order to prevent the unit from reversing its cycle during the night.

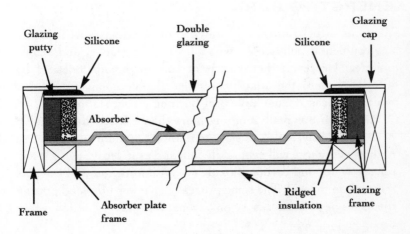

Cross-section of modular wall unit

Solar clothes dryer

With a little modification, the external modular wall air heater can be used to construct a clothes dryer that requires no electricity. Construct the heating unit as already described and fit with a low-amperage or solar-powered fan in the upper vent. Behind the wall heater, inside the laundry, build an insulated drying cupboard. Place a removable water drip-tray on the floor inside the cupboard and install clothes-drying racks.

When the sun's rays strike the absorber panel of the wall air heater, the air behind it is heated, which then rises and enters the drying cupboard through the top vent. More air is drawn through a bottom vent in the wall heater, becomes heated, and the cycle continues. The delivery of air into the drying cupboard is assisted by the fan.

This type of system will only be effective if the outside solar collector is fitted to a north-facing wall (a south-facing one in the northern hemisphere). If this is not possible because of the location of your laundry, the drying cabinet should be constructed in another room that faces north.

ENERGY TO BURN

Wood as a fuel source still draws a lot of criticism as being an environmental polluter — wood fires make smoke, and smoke pollutes. However, the amount of carbon dioxide released by wood fires into the atmosphere is negligible compared to that which is released from huge coal-burning power stations.

A wood fire is really nothing more than a speeded-up version of natural decay, and is as close to natural pollution as there is. In nature, every tree will eventually fall, and as it decays away it will release water and carbon dioxide (CO_2) into the air and leave its minerals in the soil. The same process as having a fire and putting the ashes in your garden — only in nature it takes a little longer.

SLOW-COMBUSTION WOOD HEATERS

Although solar heating is an effective and economical means of warming our homes when the sun is shining, we also need to cater for overcast days and cold nights. Wood-fire heating is possibly the oldest and most effective way of warming a house, apart from the sun.

Slow-combustion wood heaters are an energy-efficient means of space heating, and used correctly will reduce your overall energy bill. There are enough designs now available to suit everyone, and not only will they radiate warmth throughout your house, but they can also be used to heat water for baths, showers and room radiators.

When shopping for a wood heater choose carefully; a heater may be aesthetically pleasing and heat up quickly, but unless it is a slow-combustion unit its heat will soon die away once you've gone to bed and can longer fuel it. A slow-combustion unit can be loaded up with wood and once the house has warmed up it can then be turned down to maintain warmth and save energy.

The best place to install your heater for maximum effect is in a room in the centre of your house. Nobody wants a heater in the middle of a room, so the next best thing is to place it near a living room wall that is closest to the centre of the house. If your heater comes with a hot-water jacket, you will be able to install hot water radiators in the bedrooms (see *Heating the house with hot water*, pages 49–51).

When installing the heater it is important that it is correctly positioned in relation to adjoining walls and that it stands on a heat-resistant base. You can purchase a ready-made slate base, or you may prefer to lay some attractive brickwork. Flue pipes should be at least 45 centimetres (17½ inches) from the wall, unless they are protected by a shield, and all joints fitted so that they are airtight. Check the manufacturer's guidelines before installation.

Heat exchangers

A heat exchanger can rescue additional heat from the flue which would otherwise be lost to the air outside. It is usually a doughnut-shaped pipe that fits into your existing flue, and flue gases simply circulate through the exchanger to direct more heat into a room. The amount of air they pull from the flue can approach 500 degrees Celsius (932 degrees Fahrenheit).

Maintaining your wood heater

The biggest drawback to using a slow-combustion wood heater is creosote build-up. When you close the heater down by limiting the amount of oxygen entering the firebox, the flames die down but the embers continue to glow, reducing the heat output and maintaining a cosy, warm climate. While this means that the heater is working at maximum efficiency, it also means that combustion may be incomplete. Several components of the wood vaporise without burning and escape into the flue as a sticky, brown substance which traps the carbon from the ascending smoke, dries out and bakes onto the inside of the flue pipe, becoming what is commonly referred to as creosote.

Once dried out, creosote is inflammable, although it takes quite a lot of heat to set it on fire. This is a rare occurrence in modern airtight wood heaters, and if a flue fire were to start it would more than likely just burn itself out. However, it is better to avoid this situation by reducing creosote build-up and hence the need for regular maintenance.

Considerable creosote build-up can be prevented by simply allowing a low fire to burn in the heater during the day with the dampers fully open. At night, fully load the heater and allow it to continue burning, with the dampers still fully open. Once the house is sufficiently warm, or just prior to going to bed, fill the firebox if necessary and allow it to burn on full flame for about 10 minutes, or until the wood is fully burning. Then, close down the dampers. Following this procedure will mean that creosote is only being produced during the time that the heater is closed down.

It is also imperative that you clean your flue on a regular basis to eliminate any creosote build-up — twice during the period of the year when the heater is in use will usually be sufficient, unless there is a continual excess build-up. Flue brushes — stiff wire bristles bound up in a twisted cable — are available from retailers of slow-combustion wood heaters in various diameter sizes to suit all flue pipes. At one end of the brush there is a loop to attach a weight, and at the other end another loop to attach a piece of sturdy rope or chain. To make a weight, hold an eyebolt, with nut attached, in the centre of an empty jam tin, fill it with wet concrete and allow it to set. Then it's just a simple matter of climbing up onto the roof, removing the waterproof flue cap, and running the brush up and down the pipe until all the creosote has fallen down. Make sure that the firebox door of the heater is closed when you carry out this job, otherwise you'll end up with a house full of creosote and soot. Lastly, shovel the creosote and any ash into a bucket and dispose of it around your garden beds.

FUEL IN THE CITY

If you live in a rural area, firewood is usually readily available. However, city-dwellers who elect to have wood heaters for winter warmth will need to use a little ingenuity in gathering firewood.

A lot of timber in the city and suburbs is regarded as waste and in most cases will be freely available to you. Old wooden hardwood pallets found in shipping yards, markets and factories are a good source. A walk along the beach or the riverbank will usually turn up pieces of driftwood. Scrap wood and hardwood offcuts can often be scrounged from timber mills, or at least purchased very inexpensively. Deadwood can also be found scattered under trees in parks and reserves — check with local authorities first, in case you need permission to take it — and loppings by council workers from neighbourhood tree prunings can be collected and seasoned for the following winter.

An occasional weekend trip to the country may also help add to your fuel supply, and if you don't mind towing a trailer you may be lucky enough to find a tonne or two of free firewood. Combine your scavenging with logs made from old newspapers and, if needed, a small supplementary load of purchased firewood, and all your fuel needs should be taken care of.

Newspaper logs

Newspaper logs make an excellent fuel for slow-combustion heaters. Roll a newspaper tightly around a broom handle, working from the bottom of the page. Tie the log with string and then soak it in cooking oil until completely saturated. When dry, roll more newspaper around it until the layer of newspaper is about 10 centimetres (4 inches) thick, and secure again with string. Paper logs will burn for several hours.

Compressed paper blocks

To make compressed paper blocks which can be used in combustion heaters, you must first soak paper in water (any kind of paper will do), pulp it, pack it into suitable moulds and compress them.

You can construct a mould from a large fruit juice tin. First draw a line around the tin 50 millimetres (2 inches) up from the bottom. Cover the space between the line and the bottom of the tin with drilled holes 3 millimetres ($\frac{1}{10}$ inch) in diameter to allow water to escape. Next cut a piece of hardwood into a circular shape a fraction smaller than the inside diameter of the mould. This is known as a 'follower'.

Pack the pulp tightly inside the mould, up to the rim, and then place the follower on top of it. Next put the mould under a sturdy shelf or bench, follower side down, and then position a small hydraulic car jack so that its base rests against the underside of the shelf, and the jacking bar against the follower. Operate the jack to compress the paper until all the water has been squeezed out. Remove the compressed paper from the mould and allow it to dry thoroughly before use.

Pine cone fire starters

If you're lucky enough to have pine trees growing nearby, or whenever you're out-and-about and happen to see any pine cones, collect them. They make great natural fire starters! Because they contain a lot of resin they will burn for a long time, and you can use just a piece of lit crumpled paper to start them burning. Hardwood up to 9 centimetres ($3\frac{1}{2}$ inches) in diameter can be placed directly on top of burning pine cones and will begin to burn in a very short time.

Fringe benefits of wood heating

Ash

Pure hardwood ash contains a little under 5 per cent potassium carbonate and about 2 per cent phosphoric acid, both of which are beneficial to your garden. Potassium is what gives growing plants strong stems, and phosphorous makes for better roots. When these two elements are combined with other mineral salts in ash they are alkaline in nature and will sweeten acid soils. Ash can be used in the same way as you use garden lime — be careful not to over-sweeten your soil though. Most garden plants prefer a pH of 6.0 to 7.0, which is nearly neutral. If in doubt, test the soil with litmus paper to see where yours fits on the pH scale.

You will also find that if you sprinkle hot ashes on the garden in early spring, when the weather is still cool, it will help to keep down weeds at the time they are most vigorous. Slugs, snails and other slimy garden pests all hate wood ash and will not go across it. Sprinkle a good layer of ash around newly planted seedlings, lettuces, or other affected plants to protect them. Ash spread liberally around the crowns of carrots, onions, leeks, beets and other root crops will discourage many species of root maggot fly from laying eggs. Young seedlings can also be protected from cutworm with wood ash — dig a 15 centimetre- (6 inch-) deep trench around the planted-out area and fill with ash.

Soot

Soot contains many of the minerals that are found in wood ash, plus about 2 per cent nitrogen. It is used in potting soil, and is also a good addition to greenhouse or indoor plant soil mixes. It makes any soil a deep, rich black colour. However, it does have an extremely strong odour, so let it age before including it in indoor plant mixes.

To make your own potting soil for growing garden seedlings, mix the soot with garden loam, peat moss and sand. For plants that don't like acid soils, add a little garden lime at least six weeks before you intend to use it. Vary the loam, peat moss and sand mix according to the plant's requirements.

HEATING THE HOUSE WITH HOT WATER

If you have a slow-combustion wood heater that has a hot-water jacket you can use hot water to warm other rooms in the house by coupling it to hot water radiators. These radiators are available as small skirting board (baseboard) units or larger standing units which look very similar to free-standing oil-filled radiators that use electricity to heat the oil.

To set up such a heating system you will need hot water radiators, a hot water storage tank and a low-amperage or solar/battery-powered pump if the distance between your radiators and your storage tank is too great for hot water to circulate effectively by convection.

In most homes the hot water tank operates as a high-pressure system, direct from supplied water. However, when using a wood heater to heat water from a storage tank it must be a low-pressure, vented system, otherwise your storage tank may explode. It is recommended that a plumber be employed to install a hot water space heating system. The following diagram illustrates how it should be laid out.

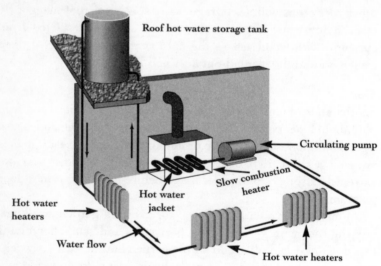

Heating the house with hot water

Slow-combustion clothes dryer

Another benefit of a slow-combustion heater or stove fitted with a hot-water jacket is that it is possible to link it to a clothes dryer that requires no electricity.

Construct a drying cupboard with insulated walls. On each of two opposite walls, construct an insulated inner wall so that a hollow air space is created. Install lower and upper vents in that wall with low-amperage or solar-powered fans on each bottom vent to circulate the air.

Install a low-pressure storage cistern in the roof (see *Solar hot water*, pages 74–85) and connect the slow-combustion stove's hot-water jacket outlet to the inlet of the storage cistern. In the base of the drying cupboard, install a spiral coil made from copper pipe. Connect the storage cistern's outlet pipe to the coil of copper pipe; the hot water passing through the pipe will warm the air in the drying cabinet. Hot water is circulated through the coil, back to the hot-water jacket and then to the storage cistern by a small low-amperage pump.

Build a false floor, perforated with holes to allow air circulation, in the bottom of the drying cupboard above the heating coil. This will provide protection against being burnt when using the cupboard. The false floor and the space beneath it should be lined with a fire-retardant material to eliminate the danger of overheating. Install hanging rods at different levels so clothes can be hung to dry.

DISTRIBUTING WARM AIR THROUGHOUT THE HOUSE

Distributing heat efficiently throughout the house is an important means of conserving energy because it means you'll need less space heating. It eliminates the problem of some rooms being hot while others are like ice-boxes.

Good air circulation is essential, especially if you have only a single heat source, and is easily achieved by the installation of fan blowers and wall vents. Small, inexpensive, low-speed, low-amperage electric fans fitted above doorways — near the ceiling where heat builds up — will direct hot air into other rooms. Fans should blow hot air through an appropriate vent in a horizontal direction and, if not coupled with an open doorway, wall vents will need to be installed at floor level. When deciding upon which doorways should be fitted with fans, choose those rooms where more heat will be required.

In a double-storey house install vents between the studs through the floor/ceiling connecting the upper and lower storeys. Hot air will rise from the lower to the upper storey through these vents, whilst cold air will sink to be heated. Fit shutters in the vents so that they can be closed off during the day, keeping the warm air in rooms that are being used. At night the vents can be opened so that warm air circulates to bedrooms upstairs. During the day, rooms with south-facing windows (north-facing in the northern hemisphere) will receive little heat. This type of fan arrangement will help to circulate warm air to such areas both day and night.

AIR-LOCK HEAT TRAP

In winter avoid using too many external doors. A good habit to get into is to restrict yourself to using only one. A more effective alternative is a simple foyer air-lock which prevents warm air from escaping and masses of cold air rushing in each time you open the door.

An air-lock is easily constructed from timber framing, lined both sides with gyprock board, the cavity insulated with natural cellulose fibre. If the air-lock is an addition to the house, its external cladding should match the outside of the house. Insulation is unnecessary. Both doors should be well sealed with weatherproof stripping and a draught excluder.

The air-lock will save heat in two ways: minimal loss of heat around the doors, and a minimal change of air when entering or leaving the house. It is important to remember not to have both doors open at the same time, otherwise your air-lock will not do its job. Install shelves and hooks on one wall for coats, shoes and rainwear.

ENERGY-EFFICIENT COOLING

There are many simple and effective ways to improve the coolness of your home during the hot summer months without using energy-hungry air conditioners. The trick is to stop heat from entering your house in the first place, rather than trying to cool the air down once it is inside.

As discussed in Chapter 1, adequate insulation is essential. In winter, hot air will try and escape; in summer the reverse is true: heat will try and get in any way it can. In addition to installing insulation, shading your house and using natural convection to pull cool air through it will reduce the need for energy-powered cooling appliances.

CAPTURING COOLING BREEZES

Wind creates a zone of high pressure on the windward side of a house and a zone of low pressure on the leeward side. By ensuring an adequate cross-flow of air through the house you can take advantage of this pressure difference and cause cool night air to flow through the house. The flow of cool night air will not only help to keep your house cool, but will also increase the rate that sweat evaporates from your skin, giving you a sense of comfort. By directing the flow of summer breezes through the house you will be provided with relief in humid conditions, and the cooling of the house in the evening.

Your house need not face directly into the breeze, as long as it is offset no more than 45 degrees either way; in other cases, a row of shrubs, or a high, continuous fence, will redirect the breeze into the house. To gain maximum benefit from cross-ventilation the breeze should be directed through smaller, low-level openings on the windward side, and then exhausted through larger openings on the leeward side.

FORCED VENTILATION

Although natural ventilation is the most ideal way of keeping cool, it will only work to your advantage when the conditions are right. However, a cooling flow of fresh air through the house can be guaranteed in all conditions by the use of fans. This type of cooling is known as forced ventilation, and in most circumstances it creates an indoor temperature that is just as comfortable as that obtained from an air conditioner, but uses far less energy.

CEILING FANS

The revolving ceiling fan not only circulates and freshens the air inside your house during summer but also helps to keep you cool by increasing the amount of moisture evaporating from your skin. Choose a low-amperage fan to reduce energy usage, or better still install a solar-operated model. Solar ceiling fans are now readily available and run on small electric motors powered by solar cell panels. They switch on automatically when the sun comes out and switch off again when the sun sets. In the evening you can then take advantage of the prevailing winds to keep your home cool.

WINDOW FANS

Window fans can be installed in existing windows and provide the most effective ventilation at minimal cost. They are designed so that their housing will fit temporarily into an existing window opening, and in most cases simply plug into a power point. However, as with a ceiling fan it is possible to use an electric motor that is connected to a solar panel/battery set-up. The batteries will guarantee night-time operation and are simply recharged during the day when the sun is shining.

The only requirement for a window fan is that the fan has a good base to rest on, so it is best to fit it so that it can be supported by the windowsill. It is also important to seal the portion of the window not occupied by the fan.

If your window fan does not have an adjustable mounting frame to seal the window you will have to make one. Cut a piece of 10 millimetre (2½ inch) plywood to fit the window opening, then cut an opening in the plywood for the fan. A felt gasket between the fan mounting and the plywood will insulate and cut down on vibration noise. You can substitute the felt with rubber door jamb sealing tape — it is adhesive on one side, which may make installation easier. Secure in place by tacking strips of 10 millimetre (2½ inch) half-round mounding flush against the window frame and the plywood panel. Finally, prime and paint the plywood panel for both weather protection and appearance.

Window fans should be installed in windows on the leeward (downwind) side of the house for maximum efficiency. A correctly installed window fan will pull cool fresh air through open windows on the windward side of the house and exhaust warm air to the outside.

Window fans will allow air to pass freely into and out of the house even when the fans are not operating. This may be undesirable in winter and during extremely hot daytime weather, so you will need to purchase or make insulated covers that will fit over the fan openings.

EXHAUST FANS

Kitchen, bathroom and general ceiling or wall exhaust fans will not only stimulate air circulation by expelling hot air, but will also eliminate unpleasant odours. If an exhaust fan is set into a wall, a single opening in the wall is all that is required. Fit a rubber insulating strip around the internal fan plate if one is not provided. A rubber gasket will also need to be fitted between the external cowling of the fan and the wall to provide a weatherproof seal.

If the fan is installed in the ceiling, airtight ducting should connect the fan housing to an external roof vent to prevent excess moisture from collecting in the roof and reduce the risk of a grease fire in the roof. A grease fire, although rare, can occur where an exhaust fan is situated above the stove.

Most exhaust fans operate from a wall switch and some include a louvre-type vent to prevent the free flow of air when it is not in use. The vent automatically opens when the fan is switched on and then closes again when it is switched off.

WHOLE-HOUSE FANS

If finances allow it, you could install a far more powerful cooling system: the whole-house fan. Installed in the ceiling, it sucks up warm air from the house and blows it out through the roof via gable vents. Cool air is then drawn in through floor vents or low external wall vents on the south side of the house (the north side in the northern hemisphere).

The fan can be powered by a solar cell panel that incorporates a storage battery for night-time use. It will then provide night comfort and daytime cooling for most of the summer.

SHADING

Proper shading is essential for a cool summer house. Because of the sun's high angle in the sky in summer, the use of pergolas, verandahs and deciduous plants is very attractive for natural cooling, particularly on northern and western aspects (southern and eastern in the northern hemisphere).

Temperature control can be as simple as growing deciduous vines, such as grape or wisteria, over a pergola, or growing espaliered trees against walls to insulate them in summer and expose them to sunlight in winter.

Shade houses make an attractive and cool retreat from soaring summer temperatures. They can be complex structures of shade cloth and lattice, or simple constructions, for example a pergola with vines growing over it and plants hanging down from it. Light reaching the house is filtered through the greenery and the hanging plants help to lower the surrounding temperature considerably through the moisture evaporating from their pots. This evaporative cooling effect can be further increased by installing a drip system: water lines are attached to the roof framework of your shade house above the plants, letting water drip slowly and constantly. As the day heats up the evaporation increases — more so on extremely hot days — greatly lowering the surrounding air temperature and increasing the cooling effect.

A shadehouse attached to the south-facing wall (north-facing in the northern hemisphere) with a water-drip system, combined with a greenhouse or sunroom on the opposite side of the house will give you summer air conditioning that will keep your home as cool as would a power-hungry mechanical device. The greenhouse acts as a solar pump, setting in motion natural convective circulation of the air inside your house. As hot air is vented through its roof, cooler air is drawn from inside the house, and then even cooler air (through strategically placed high vents) from the shadehouse.

MAKING THE MOST OF PLANTS

Deciduous plants

Trees are natural air conditioners! It's always cool beneath a tree because their leaves block out solar radiation and release water into the air. Deciduous trees should be an integral part of landscape planning as they help maintain an energy-efficient home. Deciduous trees located mostly to the east or west of the house, not directly in front of a north-facing wall (a south-facing wall in the northern hemisphere), will create the maximum amount of shade to cool the house in summer but will still allow sunlight to penetrate and warm the house in winter. A row of trees may also be planted to channel cool breezes to the house in summer, and also to deflect cold winds away in winter.

They are also effective during cooler spring and hotter autumn weather. In early spring, when the rays of the sun may still be important for warming the house, their small leaves don't block much of the sunlight, while in late autumn, when in many areas it is still quite warm, their leaves continue to provide shade.

When planting trees that will eventually grow quite large, make sure that they are situated far enough away from the house so that branches and roots won't become a problem. Growing habits must also be taken into account to avoid long shadows being cast onto your house during winter.

Other deciduous plants, such as grapes, are useful if grown on the western side of the house (eastern in the northern hemisphere) on a high, free-standing pergola or trellis above window height. The leaves of the grape vines will also provide a valuable mulch in autumn.

Cool evening breezes can be deflected into the house in summer by a high, continuous, free-standing trellis of deciduous plants. Again, grow grapes or any of the other rambling vine or cane fruits: passionfruit (*Passiflora* spp.) and loganberry or boysenberry (*Rubus loganobaccus*).

Living blinds

Plants can be used to form living blinds for your windows to cool the house and fill it with a cool, greenish, broken light.

Windows can be shaded by window pergolas. A window pergola is no more than an extended window box with lattice or individual lengths of wire running from it to the top of the window frame. Crops such as climbing beans will provide shade, as well as being a nutritious food source. In winter, flowers can be planted, providing a splash of colour while allowing the sun's warmth to penetrate.

Portable living blinds

Portable planter boxes on rollers make ideal window shades that will provide cool green screens for windows facing the hot summer sun. They can also be positioned to redirect cooling wind currents into the house during the evening.

In winter they can be placed in front of south-facing windows or walls (north-facing ones in the northern hemisphere) to give protection and insulation against cold winds. A pocket of still air is formed between the dense foliage and the window or wall, diminishing the ability of the wind to steal the heat.

Portable planter boxes should be constructed from a weatherproof material such as treated pine, and can be as large as you wish. However, bear in mind that it is easier to move or adjust several small planters than one gigantic one — as a general rule of thumb, because of the weight of soil, a practical maximum length would be about 1.5 metres (5 feet). The planter should also have an appropriate frame to hold up wires for climbing plants.

When choosing your plants or vines, select from varieties that are tolerant to both hot and cold weather, and that will provide plenty of dense foliage all year round.

Living window awnings

A living window awning is much like a living blind, except that a framed pergola-like awning is built to extend out from above the window, just below the eave. The length of the overhang should only need to be about 60 centimetres (23½ inches) and it should be constructed from weather-resistant material.

Unlike the living blind, which is designed to support small vine crops, the living awning is best suited to plants such as kiwi fruit (*Actinidia chinensis*), grape (*Vitis* spp.), *Wisteria* spp., *Clematis* spp., etc. It will provide a cool, green shade in summer and interesting branch patterns to look at through the window, and will allow sunlight to penetrate in winter.

Lawns and hedges

Simple climate modifiers such as lawns, plants and water evaporation, will not only cool down your living environment but will make it attractive and comfortable. The good old suburban lawn has a lot going for it as a climate modifier because combined with other greenery around your house it has a definite cooling effect. Traditional lawns, however, use up an unacceptable amount of precious water resources, and can also be very labour-intensive to maintain, so try replacing it with a drought-hardy thyme lawn (*Thymus* spp.), *Dichondra* spp., or lawn camomile (*Matricaria* spp.) if you live in a cool area.

Paths, paving, large expanses of concrete, and bitumen roads all contribute to heat build-up and discomfort from harsh reflected light. Hedges can be planted to eliminate road glare, and paths eliminated and replaced by paving stones with ground-cover plants such as thyme (*Thymus* spp.), camomile (*Matricaria* spp.), moneywort (*Lysimachia nummularia*) and pennyroyal (*Mentha pulegium*) growing between them. As the plants spread, the glare of the stones is reduced and eventually eliminated. Try different varieties of thyme — caraway, woolly, magic carpet, Doon Valley and Shakespear — combined with camomile for a variety of colour, and wormwood (*Artemisia absinthium*) or yew (*Taxus* spp.) for a tall hedge.

WINDOW SHADING

In summer, all windows except those that face south (north in the northern hemisphere) should be shaded. Solar heat gain through windows and sliding glass doors can be greatly reduced if drapes, blinds, shutters and shades are closed when the sun is shining on them.

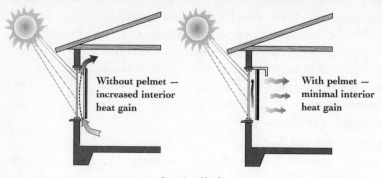

Without pelmet —
increased interior
heat gain

With pelmet —
minimal interior
heat gain

Interior Shade

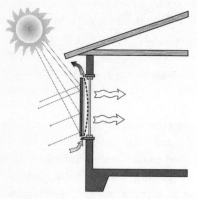

Exterior shade — little or no heat gain

In summer, it is good to get into the habit of closing all curtains or shades on east-facing windows at night to prevent morning sun from entering. By mid-morning the north-facing windows (south-facing in the northern hemisphere) should be covered, and the west windows by early afternoon. This rotation effectively helps reduce heat gains; on the other hand if the weather is extremely hot, close all drapes or shades and only open them once the sun has set.

However, unless your internal shades have an insulated backing, only a very small amount of heat is reflected back, the rest is trapped inside. It is much more effective to shade your windows on the outside. External shades, such as roll-up awnings, are an effective and efficient way of stopping heat gain through windows.

If you're short on cash, the cheapest and simplest method of exterior shading is to hang a canvas or bamboo blind outside the window, from a roof overhang. Leave a space for venting at the top to prevent a pocket of hot air from building up. At night the shade can be rolled up to allow cooling breezes to enter, and in

ched to that side of the house it will constantly shade the walls
inter, making the inside of the house quite cool and gloomy.
golas, or verandahs that have open roofing (bare rafters),
ch allow winter sun penetration, are the better alternative for
side of the house. Verandahs on west-facing walls will heat up
iderably during the long hot summer afternoons, making
h uncomfortable to occupy; however, they do have the
antage of providing some heat-gain protection for west-facing
lows. The eastern and southern (or northern in the northern
isphere) sides of the house are ideally suited to verandahs,
will be cool and comfortable during the heat of summer.

RGOLAS

verandahs, pergolas are extremely popular as outdoor living
s. If attached to a north-facing wall (south-facing in the
hern hemisphere) a pergola will exclude the hot summer sun
dmit winter sun.
have already briefly indicated how you can turn a pergola into
l summer retreat by growing climbers over it (see *Living
w awnings*, pages 58 and 59). However, in some situations it
not be desirable to grow climbing plants over it, or
atively you may wish to have greater control over
rating sunlight. In that case, adjustable louvres are ideal for
olling the sun's rays both in summer and winter, and
ctly orientated they can be fine-tuned from morning until
fternoon. Their use is not just limited to the pergola, they can
d as adjustable screen fences as well.
maximum sun control, the louvres should ideally align
south — that way they can be adjusted accordingly to suit
c of the sun. Use a compass to make sure that the louvres
rrectly aligned.
make your louvres, follow the instructions for building your
kylight louvres (see pages 24 and 25). The only difference
king skylight and pergola louvres is their size.

F VENTING

ation is a simple method of cooling which utilises natural
ction to draw hot air from within your home and replace it

winter it can be taken down and stored away. If wind is a problem
where you live it will be necessary to provide a ground anchor —
preferably one with an elastic shock cord — to prevent flapping.

Another option that has become increasingly popular for solar
control is tinted or reflective film applied to the inside of the
window glass. It is highly effectively in keeping the heat of the
summer sun out, but unfortunately the same applies in winter —
if fitted on north-facing windows it will prevent much-needed
warming sunlight from entering the house. It is permanent and
cannot be removed during winter. However, on east- and west-
facing windows, where there is usually insufficient roof overhang
to provide adequate protection, reflective film is worth
considering. If you do consider it worthwhile, choose the most
reflective film and one that has a shading coefficient of at least 0.3.

Drapes and blinds

Drapes and other interior shades will have little effect in reducing
internal heat gain unless there is a tight seal between them and the
window frame. Only if they are well-designed will they eliminate
the possibility of a convection loop heating the house and provide
effective control of direct-gain and conductive-gain heat.

The most commonly used interior shades are Venetian and
vertical blinds, holland (roller) blinds and various types of
drapes. They do very little to exclude heat and only provide a
shading coefficient one-quarter to one-half as efficient as wide
eaves, pergolas and other exterior shading. This problem can be
solved by using interior drapes and shutters designed especially
for solar control.

Drapes should have a lining of insulating material that has a
highly reflective surface and a high resistance to conductive heat
flow. They should have a tight-fitting box pelmet at their head,
and they should fit tight up against the window frame and go all
the way to the floor. However, this level of efficiency will admit
little, if any, light, so the interior of your home will be quite dark.

Drapes are more effective when combined with other solar
controls. Keep the drapes closed during the day on east- and west-
facing windows, and use pergolas, roller awnings, or any of the
previous suggestions to exclude unwanted heat gain. Solar-

efficient drapes on north- and south-facing windows can be drawn at night during winter to prevent heat loss.

Another alternative is to install insulated holland (roller) blinds and fit a closed-in pelmet above them and closed-in guide rails down each side of the window frame. This will ensure a snug fit and seal the edges when the blinds are closed. Most readily available solar blinds are attractive and very effective, however they can be expensive to buy.

If you have the time, enthusiasm and a little expertise you may wish to make your own blinds, but remember, design is important to their effectiveness. The basic blind should consist of two layers of quilted fabric with a layer of reflective aluminium foil-fabric sewn in between them. If you have access to old holland (roller) blinds you can recycle the roller mechanism, otherwise you will have to purchase it.

Accurate measurements are of paramount importance to ensure that your blind operates smoothly. The two critical measurements are the height and width of the window. This may sound simple enough, but not all windows are perfectly symmetrical. Take measurements of both the height and width at a number of places and use the widest measurement. The blind can be trimmed later to compensate for any irregularities in the shape of the window.

You will also need to take into account the amount of material taken up by the roller. It is better to overestimate, and be able adjust the length later, than to have a blind that is too short.

It is also wise to mount your blinds outside the existing window trim, so as to avoid the problem of having to adapt mountings to different window styles. This way you can keep all your home-made blinds uniform, which will further reduce their overall cost.

Shutters

Shutters are extremely efficient at keeping unwanted heat from penetrating the house through the windows, and if insulated they can be closed tight in winter to keep the warmth in. The flexibility of their design allows an almost infinite control over solar heat gain while still allowing free-flowing ventilation.

However, to work effectively they will usually need to be adjusted several times during the day, which can become a

nuisance. This is probably the reason for their la
but don't be discouraged if you feel that they
circumstances.

A friend of mine who is a computer nut, to s
who usually goes overboard in everything he do
on his north-facing windows so that they were fu
connected control rods to each louvre, whic
attached to small electric motors controlled by
wrote a special computer program which switch
to adjust the louvres at two-hourly intervals acc
arc in the sky each week at his latitude. Now, m
a little bizarre, but it is extremely effective an
can be done with a little ingenuity.

THE SHADY VERANDAH

I still have fond childhood memories of lying b
on my parents' verandah, letting the world dr
lost in fantasy. It was a great place to relax
evenings and just listen to the sounds of the
conversation. And if the summer evenings were
camp out there. Ah yes, verandahs . . . in all
whether a patio, deck, balcony or humble lean
synonymous with an outdoor way of life.

Some verandahs fit into the overall design
others are no more than a lean-to extension
Regardless of what they look like they prov
the sun and rain, and provide a cool, shady ou
hot weather.

When houses weren't crammed together
verandah was a front-row seat to nature. T
have no verandah at all, or if they do, t
inadequate for any outdoor use, as is often th
project homes which provide token veranda
they are too narrow, face the road and hav
except for the front door.

Placement of a verandah is a vital conside
it is really quite ridiculous having one exte
facing wall (or a south-facing wall in the n

with cool air from outside. Although ceiling insulation significantly reduces heat gain from a hot roof, venting of the roof, eaves, ceiling and floor will further reduce the discomfort of summer heat. Good roof ventilation lowers the mean radiant temperature of the ceiling facing the interior of your home, making it cooler.

CONTINUOUS RIDGE VENTS

A continuous vent along the ridge of the roof, with soffit air intakes under the eaves, is by far the best venting system. As the roof heats up during the day a convective flow starts, and hot air is discharged through the ridge vent and replaced by cooler air drawn up through the soffit vents. On north-facing walls (south-facing in the northern hemisphere) it is essential to have some form of wide overhang to keep the air cool.

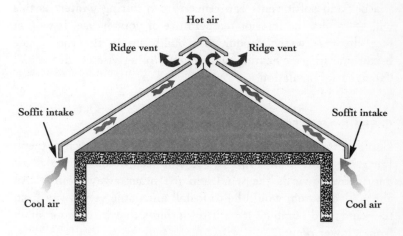

Continuous ridge vent

At night, ceiling and floor vents can be opened to draw cool air from the crawl space into the house, up to the roof space and out. You need no more than simple, screened vents placed in the ceiling and floor in several locations around the house.

The chief advantage of this continuous venting system is that the vent is directly at the apex of the roof, so hot air will continue to rise with or without a breeze being present. Because it stretches the whole length of the roof ridge, it will also allow ventilation throughout the whole of the roof space. The soffit vents provide access on both the windward and leeward side, so whatever the direction of the wind, the system can always vent toward the negative pressure at the ridge vent.

Continuous roof vents are relatively easy to install. However, if it is impractical to install continuous ridge venting in your roof, a cupola or a circulating thermal vent stack (available from most hardware stores) will help. To make them really effective you will still need soffit vents.

As a general rule of thumb, the amount of space you will need to provide for the continuous ridge vent is about 1 per cent of the total ceiling area of the house, and similarly for soffit vents. For ceiling and floor vents use the same sizing rule, and make sure that they can be closed off in winter with tight-fitting insulated panels.

Roof and soffit vents can remain open during winter, as this will not affect the interior temperature of your house. It will, in fact, disperse water vapour that builds up in the roof space because of interior heating, which could otherwise condense and damage roof insulation.

GABLE VENTS

Gable vents work best when the wind is blowing towards them. For gable vents to be effective you will need to install two vents, one facing towards the wind and the other away from it. An alternative system would be to install one gable vent away from the wind, and combine it with soffit vents that bring cool air in from a lower point.

All gable vents should be installed as close to the ridge of the roof as possible, because this is the point at which the hottest air gathers. Where natural convection is not sufficiently effective, roof fans can be installed in conjunction with the vents to discharge hot air.

When installing this, or any other type of roof vent, cover the inner side of the vent with suitable screening to prevent insects, rodents, possums and any other unwanted visitors from gaining entry to the roof space.

WIND TURBINES

The principle on which wind turbines operate is very simple: a slotted, free-turning ball on top of a vent creates a vacuum as it turns. As the speed increases so does the vacuum, sucking out a corresponding volume of air from inside the roof, or the house if the vent is connected directly to an inside ceiling. Even though wind turbines are most effective when there is a strong breeze, they will still ventilate by natural thermal action when the air is still.

A turbine vent is equally effective no matter which direction the wind is coming from, so it can be installed anywhere on the roof. However, when venting the roof space only, it should be placed as close as practical to the ridge.

LOW-PROFILE VENTS

Low-profile vents, which blend in with the roof line, have become quite popular over recent years because of their more aesthetic appearance. Unlike other venting systems they depend heavily on wind action creating a slight negative pressure on the leeward pitch of the roof to enable them to work. For this reason they need to be installed on the leeward roof slope to be effective.

DOUBLE-ROOF COOLING SYSTEM

This type of cooling system is best suited to a house that includes a clerestory in the roof, although any roof, provided its pitch is not too steep, could be modified. Because of the major structural modifications that are required, this system may only be cost effective when constructing a new house.

The principle is quite simple: the roof on the rear portion of the house is removed and replaced with insulated iron, such as square-ribbed roofing iron. Above this a second roof is constructed, leaving a gap of approximately 150 millimetres (6 inches) between the two roof surfaces. The double roof is vented so that during the day cool air can be drawn from the rear of the house through soffit vents under the eaves and discharged out through vents on the ridge of the roof. At night the soffit vents are closed. The outer roof rapidly radiates heat into the night sky, and as the air between the two roofs cools, the cooled air is allowed to enter the house through roof–ceiling vents.

SOLAR AIR CONDITIONING

Solar air conditioning is a simple and effective means of natural cooling. Like the attached greenhouse, it is a passive system that works entirely by natural convective ventilation boosted by the power of the sun. It is easily constructed and installed, and is an alternative when it is impractical or undesirable to construct a more elaborate cooling system. Over the years I have built a number of these units, and always with great success. For maximum efficiency you should install at least three or four of these units if possible.

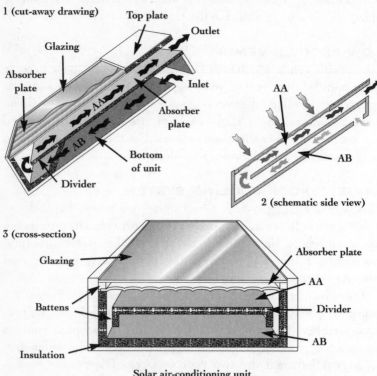

1 (cut-away drawing)

Top plate

Outlet

Glazing

Absorber plate

Inlet

AA

Absorber plate

AB

Bottom of unit

Divider

AB

2 (schematic side view)

3 (cross-section)

Glazing

Absorber plate

AA

Battens

Divider

AB

Insulation

Solar air-conditioning unit

The solar unit, which is similar in appearance to a solar absorber plate used to heat water, sits on the roof parallel to and just below the line of the ridge. Its inlet opening (see diagram 1) is connected by ducting to a closeable vent in the ceiling. Cool air is drawn through the house from the outside via vents in a south-facing wall (north-facing in the northern hemisphere), adjacent to a shade house (if practical), or preferably from vents in the floor, at the rear of the house, connected to the crawl space.

The size of the outlet vents where they are cut into the ceiling should be, in total, approximately 1 per cent of the total ceiling area of your house, although this is not critical for the units to work effectively. Likewise, the same formula applies for the floor vents. Make sure that both the floor and ceiling vents can be closed off in winter with tight-fitting insulated panels.

Construct the roof unit from 15 millimetre- ($^{3}/_{5}$ inch-) thick, exterior grade, waterproof plywood. To begin, make a base and four sides; glue and nail for added strength. Affix battens along the inner frame edge to support both the channel divider and the absorber plate (see diagram 3). Line the inside base and either side of the channel divider with rigid foam insulation, which is important for the reduction of heat loss while the system is operating. Fix the channel divider, which is 150 millimetres (6 inches) shorter than the length of the unit (see diagram 1), so that there is at least a 100 millimetre (4 inch) gap between it and the absorber plate, and at least a 100 millimetre (4 inch) gap between it and the bottom of the unit.

Corrugated iron should be used for the absorber plate, since it has a greater surface area than flat metal sheeting. Paint it matt black on both sides with at least three coats and fit it into place so that its channels will be parallel with the air flow. Allow a 3 millimetre ($^{1}/_{10}$ inch) space all around and a 30 millimetre ($1^{1}/_{5}$ inch) gap between it and the glass.

Cut the top plate (see diagram 1) from the same material as the rest of the unit and nail into position; its width should be approximately 10 per cent of the length of the unit. Set glass, at least 3 millimetres ($^{1}/_{10}$ inch) thick, allowing 2 millimetres ($^{1}/_{10}$ inch) space all round, and fix with beading. Seal between the glass and frame edge with silicone sealant, cover with storm moulding that has a 45 degree bevel to the outside, and finally seal all cracks, seams, joints and nail holes to prevent water entry and heat loss.

Position the absorber so that it faces north, with no more than a 10 degree variation either way, and is inclined to the horizontal at an angle equal to the latitude plus 5 to 10 degrees.

ATTACHED GREENHOUSE

A greenhouse attached to a north-facing wall (a south-facing wall in the northern hemisphere) is no more than a solar heat pump, and can therefore be used effectively to keep your home cool in summer. It works on the same principle as the solar air conditioning unit, drawing cool air from vents in a south-facing wall (a north-facing wall in the northern hemisphere), or from under the crawl space through floor vents at the southern end of the house (the northern end in the northern hemisphere), and expelling hot air through vents in the roof of the greenhouse. (See *Attached greenhouse*, pages 27–37.)

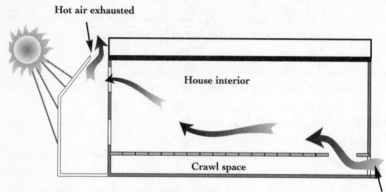

Hot air exhausted

House interior

Crawl space

Attached greenhouse for natural cooling

Cool air in

THE SOLAR CHIMNEY

The solar, or thermal, chimney is a variation of the solar air conditioning unit. It was my first experiment in building a solar heat pump, and although extremely effective it is not as aesthetically appealing as the flat plate collector. Like the flat plate collector it is a passive system that works entirely by natural convective ventilation that is boosted by the sun. As the solar chimney heats up, warm air is convected out of the top through a turbine vent, drawing cool air from vents in the floor or a south-facing wall (a north-facing one in the northern hemisphere). It is important to also vent internal walls near the ceiling, so as to maintain maximum air flow through the house. In large houses you may need to install more than one chimney. There is no reason why their design, or the materials used, cannot match that of your home.

Your solar chimney can be constructed with treated pine framing. It should be square-shaped, with glazing on the sides facing east, west and north (south in the northern hemisphere). At the top it needs to have a waterproof galvanised cap fitted with a wind-turbine vent. Lightweight aluminium or galvanised flat iron can be used on non-glazed surfaces, and all joints, screw holes and glazing must be adequately sealed with a silicone sealant so that it is both watertight and airtight. The chimney must also be flashed so that it is absolutely watertight where it enters the roof.

Fit the chimney into the roof as close as possible to a north-facing wall (or a south-facing one if you live in the northern hemisphere). Connect it to the house by a shaft that extends from the base of the chimney to the ceiling. An insulated ceiling panel can be used to close it off during winter.

You will find that a solar chimney will keep your house cool during the heat of summer. However, for it to work efficiently you must also practise good solar management: shade windows from direct summer sun; ensure that the house is adequately insulated; and install roof and soffit vents.

EVAPORATION

The evaporation of water can have a very powerful cooling effect. When water changes to water vapour it absorbs a great deal of heat; a good flow of air increases the rate of evaporation and the degree of cooling. You will experience this effect if you swim on a windy day — as you step from the water the wind evaporates the water on your skin, producing an almost instant chilling effect.

ROOF SPRAY EVAPORATIVE COOLING SYSTEM

Wetting down the roof of the house on a hot summer day works in exactly the same way. As the water spray is evaporated from the hot roof, it draws accumulated heat from the interior roof space and helps to cool down the inside of the house. My first memory of this phenomenon was when I was about seven or eight years old. It was a terribly hot summer, and I was staying at my grandmother's house. Each afternoon she would spray down the iron roof with a hose. When I asked her why she was watering the house, she said: 'keeping it cool, darling'. Although I had no idea then why watering the roof cooled the house, I certainly felt the effects.

A roof spray evaporative cooling system can easily be constructed by the home handyperson. In this system, a small amount of water is sprayed out onto the roof from small spray-jets attached to lengths of piping running along the roof. As the water sprays onto the roof, heat from the roof is absorbed and dispersed into the atmosphere as the water evaporates.

To construct your roof cooling system, mount lengths of 20 millimetre- (¾ inch-) diameter PVC pipe along the entire length of the top of your roof on either side of the ridge. Then lay more PVC pipe parallel to the ridge pipe at up to approximately 2 metre- (6½ foot-) intervals, towards the eaves for extremely large roofs. Seal one end of the pipes with PVC caps and connect the opposite end to the two pipes running either side of the ridge. Connect the two main lengths of pipe on either side of the roof ridge to a single length of pipe at one end of the roof, and connect it to your cold water supply. Purchase spray jets from a hardware store or irrigation supplier and screw them into the PVC roof piping at 2 metre (6½ foot) intervals.

The whole system is controlled by a timer switch, a solenoid valve and a thermostat (available from hardware stores) placed inside the roof space just beneath the outer roof covering.

The timer switch allows to you to determine the most suitable times for the system to be running — usually from about mid-morning to sunset in the middle of summer — and the solenoid valve and thermostat allow you to determine at what internal roof temperature the water will spray onto the roof and for how long.

As a general rule of thumb, the system should be set to commence operating at about 32 degrees Celsius (90 degrees Fahrenheit). When the thermostat senses that the roof temperature has risen over that temperature, the solenoid valve opens, water flows into the PVC pipe and a mist of water is sprayed onto the roof. The system shuts off again once the temperature falls below 32 degrees Celsius (90 degrees Fahrenheit) — usually after about 15 seconds — and will not switch on again until the temperature rises. (You can adjust the thermostat to whatever temperature you feel is appropriate for your needs.) There will be no excessive runoff or dripping because the fine spray will thoroughly wet the roof then evaporate.

The amount of electricity required to operate the timer switch and solenoid valve is negligible; in fact it can quite easily be powered by a small solar cell panel. Water consumption is also low. In areas where winters are very cold, water could freeze in the pipes, so the whole system should be drained at the end of summer to prevent damage occurring.

A roof cooling system, although not entirely passive, is a cost-effective means of keeping your home cool and enabling other passive cooling systems to work much more effectively.

NATURAL WATER-COOLED AIR CONDITIONING

This is, without doubt, one of the easiest methods of cooling. It simply involves placing large pots of water below windows where the draught will flow over them and provide natural evaporative cooling. (The pots need to be covered with insect-proof wire to prevent mosquitoes from breeding.) Alternatively, put a layer of dirt in a few medium to large, round goldfish bowls, plant some water plants, fill with water, and place below windows where a breeze will blow across the top of them. Fish ponds underneath pergolas and in a line close to access doors will have the same effect.

SOLAR ENERGY ALTERNATIVES

Your ability to maximise your use of the sun's energy will depend largely upon having a properly orientated and unshaded solar collector surface. It is important that when installing solar collectors they will not be shaded by surrounding buildings, trees and fences, and that they can be correctly positioned. Since most domestic solar systems are attached to the roof there will generally be few shading problems.

If you live in higher altitudes, locating solar collectors away from shade can be more difficult. This is because, in winter, the lower angle of the sun causes nearby objects to cast very long shadows. For example, on a steep south-facing slope (north-facing in the northern hemisphere) the hill itself can become the shading object and prevent little, if any, sun reaching a north-facing collector surface (south-facing in the northern hemisphere). In contrast, a north-facing slope (south-facing in the northern hemisphere) can be advantageous as it will help to minimise the effect of any surrounding trees or buildings located north of the collector surface.

Before commencing any solar modifications to your home, however, it is important to observe any shading that may occur, especially during winter. This will allow you to place solar collectors appropriately — in some cases it may mean the removal of trees. It is also important to remember that when planting deciduous trees for summer shade, eventually their bare trunks and branches may cause shading problems.

SOLAR HOT WATER

Climatic conditions in many parts of the world, and especially in most parts of Australia, make the solar hot water system a sensible, practical and inexpensive approach to providing domestic hot water. It is clean, costs nothing to run and requires no maintenance.

The water heater consists of a fixed, flat solar absorber on the roof, an insulated water storage tank and insulated connecting pipes. It works on the thermosiphon principle: warm water rises over colder water. As the water passing through the absorber heats up its density decreases; it rises, as heavier cold water pushes it up from beneath, and goes along the transfer pipe to the storage tank. This flow continues until the water fails to gain energy from the sun. The tank must be situated above the level of the absorber for the system to work. Since hot water cannot seek a higher level, it remains stable in the tank until needed.

Commercially manufactured units are readily available, either with a storage tank mounted directly above the absorber, forming an integral unit, or as two separate components. The latter is far more aesthetically pleasing as it allows the tank to be mounted in the roof out of sight; it can also be more effectively insulated.

THE ECONOMIC BENEFITS

Taking advantage of free energy from the sun and converting it into useable heat is a process most people understand. However, many of us still do not comprehend the most efficient way in which to use this energy within the home. Apart from heating the spaces inside our homes, the most practical use of this free sunlight is to provide domestic hot water.

Both gas and electric domestic hot water systems can run up enormous bills, depending on consumption levels, even when installed as off-peak systems. It has been established that two-thirds of the heat energy required to run a hot water system in an average year can be supplied by solar radiation. This means that an electricity-boosted solar hot water system will reduce your power consumption by two-thirds, compared with an electric off-peak water heater. If your solar heater is coupled with a slow-combustion space heater, your power consumption for hot water will be nil. In a very short time the cost of installing the solar system will be fully recovered through these savings.

Solar domestic hot water systems are among the most cost effective of residential solar applications. For this reason alone, every home owner should, where practical, take advantage of this free energy from the sun and reduce the overuse of fossil fuels.

CONSERVING ENERGY

If you do have an electric or gas hot water system, the quickest and easiest way to conserve energy yet still maintain a reasonably hot water supply, is to simply turn down the thermostat. Solar water heaters, however, do not have thermostats, unless boosted with an auxiliary electric heating element.

Solar systems that are coupled with slow-combustion heaters will deliver hot water at an acceptable temperature — one that our bodies feel comfortable with when showering — in winter and summer. When you use the solar absorber plate to warm the water during summer, it will not be as hot as that supplied by the slow-combustion heater during winter. However, it will *seem* to be the same because of the way our bodies react to atmospheric temperature variations during summer and winter.

Much energy can also be saved by putting additional insulation around your storage tank and the connecting hot water pipes. Insulation of the storage tank is especially critical for reducing energy wastage. If water stays constantly hot within the tank, replacement water will heat up very quickly, and on overcast days the use of auxiliary heating may be unnecessary or only minimal.

Wrapping your storage tank in a 150 millimetre- (6 inch-) thick insulation blanket will make it extremely energy efficient. You can protect the insulation material by constructing a simple outer cover, or cylinder, from lightweight aluminium sheeting (similar to that used in above-ground swimming pools), and fitting a cap from the same material to either end. The advantage of using lightweight aluminium is that it can be easily drilled and pop-riveted together by any competent handyperson.

A HOME-MADE SOLAR HOT WATER SYSTEM

A home-made solar hot water system is within the means of most home handypersons, and can usually be constructed quite inexpensively.

The absorber

You can build your own solar absorber plate, however precision and accuracy is absolutely essential for the unit to function. It is far easier to buy a ready-made absorber plate and adapt it to your system. A number of manufacturers now supply absorbers on their own, and though it's not quite do-it-yourself you will save considerably on the cost of purchasing a complete system.

If you are determined to build the entire unit yourself, the solar absorber is constructed as follows. For convenience of handling and to make it easier when lifting it onto the roof I would recommend that the solar absorber be built as two separate units, each 1800 millimetres ($70\frac{4}{5}$ inches) long by 1200 millimetres ($47\frac{1}{5}$ inches) wide by 120 millimetres ($4\frac{7}{10}$ inches) deep. Each unit must have a minimum net glazed area of 2 square metres ($21\frac{1}{2}$ square feet).

Each unit is relatively simple to construct, consisting of a timber-framed absorber box of the dimensions listed above, with beading on the inside of the frame to support double glazing. It must be adequately insulated with a rigid insulating material on the sides and base. When attaching the beading it should be positioned so as to allow sufficient space for the thickness of two glass panels and a 25 millimetres (1 inch) air space between them (the glass panels are fitted last).

The absorber plates are constructed from 24-gauge copper sheeting, large enough to fit snugly inside each absorber box. Attached to each absorber plate are the header and vertical riser pipes, which form a framework through which the water travels. Header pipes are made from copper pipe with a diameter of 25 millimetres (1 inch) and the vertical riser pipes are made from copper pipe 13 millimetres ($\frac{1}{2}$ inch) in diameter. The pipe framework should also fit snugly inside the absorber box, with the header pipes secured approximately 3 centimetres ($1\frac{1}{10}$ inches) from the top and bottom edges of the absorber plate. Vertical riser pipes are connected to the header pipes with capillary T fittings at approximately 150 millimetre (6 inch) intervals, with the end pipes 50 millimetres (2 inches) in from each side edge. One end of the top header pipe is capped, as is the diagonally opposite end of the lower header pipe. It is imperative that all joints are watertight.

When the pipe framework is complete it can then be attached to the absorber plate. Lay the framework on the absorber plate in its correct position and with a flat-bladed screwdriver, or other marking device, lightly score the shape of the framework on the plate. Run a screwdriver handle that is a little larger than the diameter of the copper tubing in the framework, along the scored area, applying just enough pressure to form a shallow indentation. The pipe framework should fit securely into these grooves.

The framework can be secured to the absorber plate with wire clamping. Drill a small hole on either side of a vertical riser, thread a piece of number 8 wire through and twist tightly together. Fix four wire clamps to each outside riser pipe and the centre riser pipe. These clamps will hold the framework in place so that it can be soldered to the absorber plate. It is important to provide a continuous fillet of solder between the plate and the copper tubing so as to give a satisfactory thermal bond.

When completed, the absorber plate can be fitted into the absorber box. It will be necessary to provide entry and exit holes for connection to the header pipes, and any gap between the connecting pipes and the box must be airtight.

Paint the entire absorber plate assembly and the inside of the box matt black; do not use a gloss paint as it will reflect sunlight. See an automotive paint supplier for a matt black paint that is used for painting motor vehicle exhaust systems, and will therefore withstand extreme temperatures. For the ardent do-it-yourselfer an acceptable and effective paint can be made by mixing together carbon black and linseed oil. Add the carbon black to the linseed oil until it reaches a paint-like consistency. Although the surface will have a slight shine to it, the difference in the performance of the absorber plate will be negligible. Fit the first glass panel and then carefully attach a second strip of beading above it. Apply a non-hardening putty or silicone sealant around the top of the upper piece of beading and position the top glass panel in place. Ensure that there are no gaps between the glass and the edge of the box — apply extra sealant if necessary.

Lastly, run a seam of silicone sealant along the edge of the box and the glass and then fit 25 x 10 millimetre (1 x $\frac{2}{5}$ inch) half-round DAR storm beading, overlapping onto the glass by about

10 millimetres (²⁄₅ inch), around all but the lower edge of the box — this will allow water to run off. The storm beading not only seals the edge but also helps to secure the glass. All gaps, cracks and nail holes should also be sealed with a silicone sealant.

Paint the outside of the box, including all timber surfaces, with a primer coat and then at least three top coats with the same matt black paint. Your absorber boxes are now ready to be installed on the roof. You will have to construct a suitable framework to hold them in position.

When connecting the pipes from your hot water storage tank, cold water is connected so that it enters at the bottom of the absorber and hot water exits at the top, on the diagonally opposite side. To link two units together, connect the hot water outlet from the first absorber to the hot water outlet of the second absorber, and connect the cold water inlet to the corresponding cold water inlet.

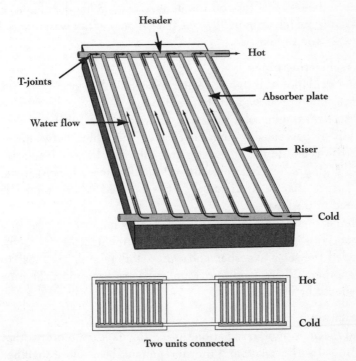

Two units connected

Solar hot water absorber unit

The water storage tank

A 400 litre (88 gallon) storage tank will provide satisfactory storage if your water consumption is around 200 litres (44 gallons) daily, which is about average for a family of four or five. This capacity allows for a reasonable carry-over of hot water for cloudy days.

Insulated copper tanks, such as those commonly used in hot water systems, are ideal and readily available new or second-hand. Additional inlet and outlet pipes for connection to the absorber plate will be necessary.

The position of the various tank connections is important, and is illustrated on page 82. The two connections to the absorber must not restrict the flow at the point of entry to the tank. Therefore, to prevent the cool water entering the tank from mixing with hot water ready for consumption, the point of entry for the flow connection from the absorber must be sited some distance below the top of the tank. As a general rule, it is satisfactory to have about 90 litres (20 gallons) of hot water stored above its point of entry.

The connecting pipes

Since circulation through the solar absorber plate occurs by the thermosiphon process, and the water must move rapidly enough to absorb maximum solar radiation without the temperature rising excessively and causing high heat losses, the piping between the solar absorber and the water storage tank must be well insulated. Use a high-grade insulation, about 25 millimetres (1 inch) thick, and ensure that it is effectively waterproofed where piping is exposed to the weather.

The size and type of pipes used is also important: use only copper with an outside diameter of 25 millimetres (1 inch), provided the solar absorber and water storage tank are close to one another. Where long horizontal runs are necessary, the pipe size should be increased.

Installation

Rapid thermosiphon circulation during the daytime requires that both the absorber plate and the storage tank be as close together as possible. However, the bottom of the storage tank cannot be closer than 600 millimetres ($23\frac{1}{2}$ inches) above the top of the absorber, otherwise reverse circulation will occur at night.

Site the absorber so that it faces due north (or due south in the northern hemisphere); a variation of 10 degrees east or west can be tolerated. The absorber must be inclined towards the horizontal at an angle equal to the latitude of the site plus 5–10 degrees. It must not be shaded by trees or other buildings between 8.00 am and 4.00 pm all year round. An examination of your site at 8.00 am, noon and 4.00 pm in June and December will reveal any possible obstructions.

The best arrangement is to site the solar absorber on the outside of the roof and the storage tank inside the roof. Piping should slope continuously upward from the solar absorber to the storage tank, without any humps where pockets of air might collect. Otherwise, the thermosiphon flow will be intermittent or may cease altogether.

Auxiliary heating

There are two ways in which auxiliary heating can be fitted to boost your system during prolonged cloudy weather. Firstly, a 2 kilowatt ($2\frac{1}{2}$ horsepower) electric element, together with a thermostat control and time switch, can be fitted to the inside of your tank. If you are using an existing off-peak electric tank as your storage tank, these devices may already have been fitted, and may therefore need only minor modification. The other alternative is to hook up the absorber in conjunction with the hot-water jacket of a slow-combustion wood heater. Under such an arrangement water is automatically drawn to the hottest source, and a continuous supply of hot water will be guaranteed.

Low-pressure system

Both gas and electric hot water systems operate as high-pressure systems, direct from supplied water. However, this is unsuitable for solar water heating, which must be converted to a low-pressure, vented system — otherwise your storage tank may explode.

The conversion is simple and only requires the installation of a small reservoir cistern, which operates in a similar manner to a toilet cistern. A ball-cock valve allows water to enter the cistern as water is drawn off to the storage tank. The top of the reservoir tank is left open, and the hot water storage tank, through a T-piece in the hot water delivery pipe, is vented into it.

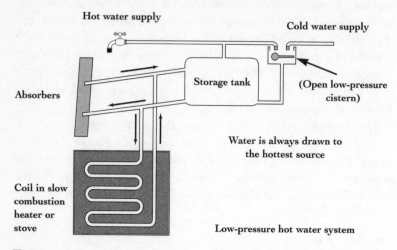

Low-pressure hot water system

Frost

People living in cold areas may have to take steps to protect their solar absorber against frost. A well-insulated cover placed over the absorber at night, and additional insulating around exposed pipes, will help to prevent water from freezing.

Corrosion

Corrosion is caused by electrolysis of materials such as galvanised pipe. To prevent this problem from occurring it is imperative that all water-carrying components, including fittings, are made of copper. Using cheaper materials is a false economy and will only shorten the life of your solar hot water system.

TRICKLE ROOF HOT WATER SYSTEM

Without doubt, a trickle roof hot water system will provide an abundance of domestic hot water in colder latitudes. A small pump circulates water around the system and up to the header delivery pipe whenever a sensor, which is fitted on the roof inside the absorber, indicates that the roof temperature is hotter than the water in the water storage tank. Water trickles out of the header pipe, down the surface of the absorber plate (where it is heated), into a collection trough, and then drains back down into the storage tank.

As water is only heated when the pump is operating, and this can only occur when the roof is hot, water in the pipes will drain back into the storage tank at night. In cold climates, therefore, this type of system has the advantage of preventing water in the pipes from freezing. However, it is disadvantaged by the fact that the pump will only work when the roof is sufficiently hot. Therefore it may be necessary to have an auxiliary heating system installed, such as an electric booster element in the storage tank, or a slow-combustion heater, for days when it is overcast.

This type of solar hot water system requires a large roof area that can be utilised as a solar collector. Before contemplating the installation of this type of system you need to assess whether or not standard absorber plates would achieve the same end result in your circumstances, and the cost-effectiveness of the installation. A trickle roof hot water system is beyond the capabilities of most home handypersons and will require the services of professional tradespeople.

Constructing a trickle roof hot water system

A trickle roof hot water system is constructed as follows. First, the north-facing side of the roof (the south-facing side in the northern hemisphere) is framed-up as if you were constructing one large absorber box, with battens running across the roof to support the absorber plate. The next step is to install adequate insulation; roofing material can be removed or the insulating material can be placed directly on top of it. Insulation is important to prevent overheating of the roof space and to keep most of the heat in the water.

Corrugated aluminium roofing, which acts as the absorber plate, is placed on top of the insulation and secured to the battens. A header delivery pipe with small holes in it is secured to the top of the absorber plate just below, and running the full length of, the ridge of the roof. Along the base of the absorber plate and above the gutter is a collection trough.

The absorber plate is painted with a temperature-resistant, matt black paint and then the whole of the framed roof area is glazed. All glazing and nail or screw holes and cracks must be sealed so they are watertight.

All fittings to the header pipe and leading from the collection trough should be copper. The water circulating pump can be powered by either low-amperage mains supply or a solar/battery unit.

GARDEN SOLAR HOT SHOWER

A simple garden shower for cleaning the dirt off the kids, or yourself after gardening, can be made by simply cutting the bases off plastic drink bottles, threading the bottles onto a garden hose, and then spreading the hose out to catch the sun. By attaching a shower rose to the end of the hose, you have a warm outdoor shower for cleaning up before entering the house.

A more permanent outdoor hot shower can be made by constructing a smaller version of the solar collector used in a solar hot water system and coupling it with a small holding tank.

HEATING A SWIMMING POOL

A solar system to heat the swimming pool is relatively simple to construct and an ideal first solar project for the home handyperson. It works on the same principle as the trickle roof hot water system (see page 82).

The simplest form of trickle heater takes advantage of the solar heat absorbed by the roof covering, be it tiles or iron. The roof itself becomes one gigantic solar collector. Water trickles down the roof from a pipe on the roof ridge, is warmed up, and either flows directly into the swimming pool, or first into a storage tank near the pool. Because of its unique simplicity there is virtually no maintenance.

When I began planning the construction of a trickle water heater for my swimming pool some years ago, everyone thought I was quite mad because the system would be open to the air, not enclosed in a glass box solar collector, so the heat loss would be enormous. Basically what they were saying was correct: a lot of heat would be lost. But the sheer size of the system (the entire roof area) made up for any deficiencies. It was, in fact, an extremely efficient system.

To construct your solar swimming pool heater, run a length of header pipe along the ridge of the roof on its northerly aspect (southerly in the northern hemisphere). Drill small holes in the pipe at regular intervals so that water will be able to trickle out and down the roof. Install a small low-amperage or solar pump, preferably where the water exits the pool, to pump water up from the swimming pool to the header pipe on the roof.

The water will trickle down from the header pipe, be heated by the sun as it runs down the roof and will collect in the guttering. By installing adjustable baffles you can prevent the heated water from running into the downpipes. Install separate exit pipes in the guttering so that the heated water can be directed into the swimming pool or a nearby storage tank. Fit a gate valve to each of the exit pipes. When you need to direct the roof water into the downpipes rather than the swimming pool, close the gate valves but open the baffles in the gutter. This system is particularly effective at preventing dirt that may have built up on the roof from clogging the pool plumbing or ending up in the pool. Simply allow the water to run into the downpipes for a few minutes so that you can start off with a reasonably clean roof.

SOLAR ELECTRICITY

If you are building a new home solar electricity may be the answer to your household energy needs. It is possible to install a solar system that will provide all your power needs, with the exception of an electric stove and freezer, at a cost comparable to what you'll pay for connection to the main power grid. Check out all the costs thoroughly before proceeding, and especially government rebates that are often available for going solar, because they can be quite substantial.

Solar electricity can also be used in conjunction with standard systems to cut power consumption in existing homes. A small solar array and storage batteries can run lights, swimming pool filter pumps, internal ceiling fans, exhaust fans and the like, all of which would mean a little less dependence on fossil fuels.

HOW SOLAR ELECTRICITY WORKS

Solar cells, or more correctly photovoltaic cells, convert the sun's light (radiant energy) directly into electricity. Heat (thermal energy) plays no part whatsoever in the process, in fact it will actually hamper the performance of the thin wafer-like material that makes up a photovoltaic cell.

The thin layers of sensitive or semi-conductor material in a photovoltaic cell are usually made from silicon crystals, doped with boron. When sunlight illuminates them a positive and a negative charge are generated. This in turn stimulates a flow of electrons across the surface of each cell, creating a small electric current.

The efficiency with which a photovoltaic cell converts sunlight into electricity is only about 15 per cent, yet each solar cell can still produce between 0.5 to 1 volt (V) of electricity in bright sunlight, and a current flow of 20 to 40 milliamps (mA), or approximately 2 amps for a 100 millimetre (2½ inch) solar cell.

To obtain sufficient power, a number of photovoltaic cells are wired together in a series and housed in a solar panel or module. A typical solar panel will contain 36 cells and be capable of producing an output of 13 to 16 volts of direct current (DC). These panels are then connected together to form what is known as a solar array system, which can, depending upon its size, produce just a few watts of electrical power or several kilowatts.

IS SOLAR ELECTRICITY RIGHT FOR YOU?

Before you embark upon designing a solar system, you must first ascertain the amount of sunlight your solar array would receive. The sun's intensity on earth is governed by two factors: the amount of atmosphere through which it must pass and the angle at which it strikes the earth's surface. Most areas in the southern hemisphere are well suited for solar electricity; however, in extremely southern or northern latitudes the intensity of the radiant light may not be sufficient to justify the cost of installation.

Additional considerations are the location of adjoining buildings, trees and any other objects that may cast shadows across the solar array for lengthy periods. Seasonal weather patterns involving temperature, cloud cover and precipitation can also reduce the overall effectiveness of solar power. The only way in which you can determine if weather is likely to inhibit the maximum available amount of radiant light is to examine long-term weather data for your district.

The electrical power consumption per day of an average home can range between 5,000 and 35,000 watt hours (Wh). To cope with such a huge demand, you would need to install a plentiful number of photovoltaic cells and harness them together into a solar array, as previously discussed.

If your needs are simple — outdoor lighting only, indoor lighting only, or maybe just household exhaust or ceiling fans — then a basic 12 or 24 volt direct current (DC) module will suit your needs. However, if you intend to go completely solar for all your power needs, including the conversion of direct current to conventional 240 volt alternating current (AC), then you will need a substantial solar array. If you choose to run a hybrid system — a mix of solar power and power from the grid or a generator — you may be able to reduce the number of panels in the array.

A solar/electricity grid hybrid system can be advantageous in areas where weather patterns reduce the amount of available sunlight for lengthy periods. This system can be even further enhanced if you run it as a duel system: when sunlight is in excess, power comes from the solar array and any excess power is directed into the grid, for which you receive a credit from the power company. Then, when it is overcast and you need to draw power from the grid, your credit is deducted from the cost of the power you use.

With recent advancements in solar electric design there is no doubt that it is capable of providing most electricity needs. However, you must first determine whether, in your particular circumstances, solar electricity will be competitive with sourcing your power from the electricity grid in terms of the benefits versus the costs. When assessing your needs you must remember that, while setting up a solar electrical system involves a substantial initial outlay, sunlight is free, and thus the operating costs are minimal. The only effective way to determine what will work best for you is to first set out a firm plan of exactly what you want to achieve with solar power.

To run lights, fans, appliances, etc, you will need to acquire photovoltaic cell modules, power-conditioning equipment, wire, inverters (to turn the DC created by the cells into 240 volt AC power), and miscellaneous interconnecting and safety devices. Therefore you will need to discuss your requirements with someone who specialises in supplying solar equipment. They will be able to ascertain what type of system is best suited to your circumstances. You can determine the economic feasibility of the system by subtracting the initial installation costs from the total long-term financial benefits. You may find that you have to adjust your initial expectations; it may be necessary to start small, using solar electricity for only part of your energy requirements, and then when finances permit gradually expand the system so that solar power fully covers all your needs.

Whatever you do, whether it is a total solar power commitment or a hybrid system, you will not only gain long-term benefits in the form of energy savings but will also be helping to reduce fossil fuel dependency.

THE NATURAL KITCHEN

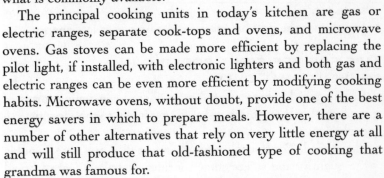

LOW-ENERGY COOKING

In most kitchens there is an amazing number of appliances to choose from, some of which are not so energy-efficient. However, many so-called kitchen-friendly products can be discarded and savings made by the careful selection and use of what is commonly available.

The principal cooking units in today's kitchen are gas or electric ranges, separate cook-tops and ovens, and microwave ovens. Gas stoves can be made more efficient by replacing the pilot light, if installed, with electronic lighters and both gas and electric ranges can be even more efficient by modifying cooking habits. Microwave ovens, without doubt, provide one of the best energy savers in which to prepare meals. However, there are a number of other alternatives that rely on very little energy at all and will still produce that old-fashioned type of cooking that grandma was famous for.

TIPS FOR EFFICIENT STOVE-TOP COOKING

The type of pots and pans you use, and the way you use them, are the keys to efficient stove-top cooking.

- Place pans on the burner or hotplate before it is turned on.
- Use high-quality pans made from cast iron, enamel or stainless steel, with thick bases, such as copper, as they heat up more quickly and retain heat better, spreading it evenly so that less energy is used to cook the food.
- Pans should be flat-bottomed and have tight-fitting lids.
- Use a pan that is slightly larger than the hotplate — don't waste energy heating a small pan on a large hotplate.
- Cook vegetables in the least possible amount of water and cook them only until they are tender, with the lid on the pot.
- Once something has boiled, turn the heat down to low and simmer.

- While a pot is on the stove lift the lid as little as possible.
- Try to make one-pot meals, cook different vegetables in a large pot with dividers, or use stackable sets of twin or triple saucepans.
- Aluminium foil under electric hotplates will reflect the heat upwards, for maximum efficiency; it also helps to keep the stove-top clean.
- Using a crockpot is cheaper than using a conventional pan on the stove-top.
- When using an electric stove, turn off the element a few minutes before the food is fully cooked.
- Use a pressure cooker or steamer to cook several things in the same pot.
- Do not use the grill for toast — a toaster uses less energy.

TIPS FOR EFFICIENT COOKING IN A CONVENTIONAL OVEN

- Roasting and baking are the most energy-consuming forms of cooking, but if meat is marinated first it will require less time to cook.
- Plan ahead. Try to cook more than one dish at a time. Double the quantity and freeze some for later, or bake a loaf of bread as you cook a casserole. Most importantly, try and use all the racks of the oven.
- Avoid opening the door, as about 20 per cent of the heat escapes each time.
- Use dark or blackened baking pans as they absorb more heat.
- Cook food in ceramic, ovenproof-glass or cast-iron casseroles, as they transfer heat more efficiently and retain it for longer.
- Turn off the oven 10 minutes before the allotted cooking time. The food will continue to cook and you'll save energy. Set the stove timer to remind you.
- Don't buy a stove that has an oven bigger than you need.

STEAMING

Steam cooking is fast, simple and energy-efficient. Food is cooked in a closed pot above boiling water, which means that it loses very little flavour and nutrition, and is tenderised and easy to digest.

Only a small amount of water needs to be heated, and once it has been brought to the boil you can turn down the heat to a simmer and enough steam will be given off to cook the food. And if you use stacked steamer containers in the one pot, you can cook a complete meal using only one hotplate.

The most efficient steamer is the bamboo type used by the Chinese. It consists of a number of circular trays stacked one on top of the other and fitted with a covering bamboo lid. The completed unit then sits in a wok partially filled with water; as the water boils, steam circulates up through the trays, cooking the food inside. It will work just as efficiently placed inside, or on top of, a saucepan of boiling water.

This simple method of cooking not only saves energy but will cook food to absolute perfection. Vegetables, fish, chicken pieces, puddings, and breads are delicious cooked this way, since dough becomes light and fluffy.

When using a steamer make sure that the water underneath it is boiling before adding the food to be cooked. Add the food, cover with a lid and reduce to a simmer. Certain foods, such as pork, may require a little extra time to cook, and you may need to top up the water occasionally. Add only water that has just been boiled in the kettle to the steamer. If you are cooking pastry or grains, wrap them in cheesecloth or muslin before placing in the steamer.

Bamboo steamers are available from Chinese grocery stores. Aluminium or stainless steel steamers, which consist of collapsible wings and fit inside a saucepan, are readily available from kitchen stores, department stores and some supermarkets.

You can of course improvise by placing a breakfast bowl upside down inside a saucepan and then sitting a plate on top of it. Once the water has boiled, place the food on the plate and put the lid on the saucepan. Another simple alternative, which I used for many years, was to place a colander over a pan of boiling water. The trick is to make sure that the outer rim of the colander rests neatly on the top edge of your saucepan and still leaves sufficient room beneath it for the water. Place the food inside the colander, cover with aluminium foil or sit the saucepan lid squarely in the top of the colander.

White wine steamed chicken

1 whole chicken, cut into pieces
2 tablespoons white wine
1 leek, finely chopped
3 slices fresh ginger
2 teaspoons herb salt
1/2 cup (4 fl oz / 125 mL) water

Place the chicken pieces in the steamer, add the leek and ginger, and sprinkle with the herb salt, wine and water. Place the steamer in a pot filled with enough water to steam for 1 hour.

This recipe is equally delicious when it is made with fish fillets, although it will need less time to cook, depending on the size of the fillets.

PRESSURE COOKING

Pressure cookers save both time and energy, and are safe and simple to use. They quickly tenderise food so that it retains its flavour and nutritional value, especially vitamin C. Most dishes usually take only one-third of the conventional cooking time when done in a pressure cooker. Most pressure cookers come with dividers so that, as with a steamer, you can cook a complete main meal altogether in one pot.

To get the most out of your pressure cooker, and to ensure that it remains in perfect working order, always follow the manufacturer's directions. When buying, always select a heavy-duty unit that will last and comes with a long guarantee.

MICROWAVE OVENS

The ability of microwave ovens to cook meals that look, taste and smell as good as those cooked in a conventional oven or on the stove is remarkable. Microwave cooking is not only an efficient way of cooking food, it is also quick, simple, easy and clean, and unlike conventional oven cooking, it doesn't require preheating. It's also downright convenient to use. Let's face it, what could be simpler than popping the food inside, closing the door, pressing a couple of buttons, and *hey presto* — food to go!

A microwave oven cooks food in approximately a quarter of the time taken by conventional methods, with energy savings of up to

70 per cent. Because of shorter cooking times, foods are not dried out or overcooked.

The principle of the microwave is very simple. A magnetron inside the oven converts electricity into microwaves. When these microwaves hit the water molecules in the food inside the oven, the water molecules vibrate at a fantastic rate. The friction caused by this vibration produces heat, which is conducted through the food to cook it.

VACUUM FLASK COOKING

A wide-mouthed vacuum flask, also known as a thermos flask, is a great energy saver. It will keep food or water hot for hours, can be used to soak dried grains, vegetables and legumes, and can even be used to cook in.

Rice and vegetable stew

Add diced vegetables, rice, lentils and stock to a saucepan. Bring to the boil, allow to boil for about 2 minutes, and then pour into a vacuum flask. Cap and leave for 3 to 4 hours to cook.

Winter breakfast

Approximately 12 hours before the time you want to eat breakfast, put 1 cup (5 oz / 155 g) of wheat or oats and 4 cups (1 litre / 1 quart) of boiling water in a vacuum flask. In the morning, strain off the liquid and serve with honey, sultanas, raisins and diced seasonal fruit. (You can soak raisins and sultanas overnight and add the soaking water to the breakfast if you wish.)

Yoghurt

Yoghurt is an excellent natural source of both protein and calcium. Unlike cows' milk, which can take up to three hours to digest, yoghurt is digested within an hour because the protein and fats in the milk are broken down by bacteria culture into simpler compounds. Because it contains no milk sugar (lactose), which many people have difficulty in digesting, it is an excellent dairy product for both young and old. People who are taking antibiotics or coming off drugs also benefit from eating yoghurt because it helps the body resist disease-causing bacteria.

Plain natural yoghurt can be made simply and quickly in a vacuum flask. Your home-made yoghurt will cost a lot less, and taste far better and fresher than the store-bought variety.

You can make it with yoghurt culture, available from most health food stores. Following the directions on the culture packet, mix the required amount with milk, heat in a saucepan on the stove to 45–55 degrees Celsius (113–131 degrees Fahrenheit), and pour into a thermos flask. Seal and leave for 3 to 4 hours. If it is not thick enough leave it for a little while longer. Pour into suitable containers and refrigerate.

Alternatively you can replace the yoghurt culture with plain natural yoghurt and prepare as follows. Heat 4 cups (1 litre / 1 quart) of milk to 75 degrees Celsius (167 degrees Fahrenheit). Let the milk cool to 55 degrees Celsius (131 degrees Fahrenheit) and add 1 cup (250 mL / 8 fl oz) of commercially produced plain yoghurt, mix well, and pour into your thermos flask. Make sure the lid is tightly secured and leave to stand for 6 to 8 hours, at which time your yoghurt should be thick enough to take out and refrigerate.

If the batch is too thin for your liking, next time try blending 1 cup (100 g / 3½ oz) of powdered milk with the warm milk before adding the plain yoghurt.

FIRELESS COOKING

I was first introduced to fireless cooking when I was a young Boy Scout and was taught how to cook casseroles and soups using a simple device known as a hay box.

A wooden box and its lid were lined with several thicknesses of newspaper (each layer glued on top of the other) and the box then filled with uncut hay. The meal was quickly brought to the boil in a billycan (a pot) over a fire. The billycan was removed from the fire and buried inside the hay-lined box. More hay was then stuffed inside a hessian bag to form a pillow, which was pushed down on top of the billycan. The lid was put back on the box and held in place with a heavy stone. The meal was prepared in the morning and left to cook in its own heat in the hay box all day. When we returned in the evening, tired and hungry, there was a hot meal waiting for us.

Today, the same principle of cooking can be employed in a modern kitchen to prepare meals and save on energy. Not only is it energy-efficient, but also a great time-saver for those who lead a busy lifestyle. A modern version of the hay box, the hot-box is simple and easy to construct. It is ideal for cooking casseroles, soups, porridge, rice, cracked wheat and other grains, dried beans, and cheaper cuts of meat that require slow and even cooking. You can also use it to keep cooked food warm and to make yoghurt. With double- or triple-stacking pots you can cook a complete meal in a hot-box.

Making a hot-box fireless cooker

Measure the pot you will be using and, using 12 millimetre-(½ inch-) thick plywood, construct a square box which is 400 millimetres (16 inches) wider than the outside diameter of your pot — this allows a 200 millimetre (8 inch) gap between each side of the box and the pot. The box must be 100 millimetres (4 inches) taller than the pot with its lid on. Use 25 millimetre (1 inch) brads (small tapered nails) and wood glue to assemble the box.

To make the lid, start with a square of plywood that overlaps the outside edge of the box by 40 millimetres (1½ inches) on each side. Cut dressed 100 x 25 millimetre (4 x 1 inch) pine (this will dress down to 90 x 19 millimetre (3½ x ¾ inch)) to fit the edges, and nail and glue the pieces in place to make a tight fit with the box.

You will need either a block of styrofoam or enough sheets of styrofoam to glue together to form a block that fits snugly inside the box and the lid space. Cut off a section of styrofoam to fit inside the lid, glue it in place, and cut out enough styrofoam to form a cavity for the pot lid. At the most, this should only be a shallow indentation. Cover the foam with aluminium foil, shiny side facing into the box, and stick down with glue.

You will now need to hollow out the remaining section of the block to fit the pot. This can be done easily by first cutting the block into quarters and cutting out the appropriate section of the pot's profile, then gluing the sections back together. Glue aluminium foil to the top and insides of the block, with the shiny side facing into the box. Glue the assembled styrofoam block in place inside the box. Use 25 millimetre (1 inch) butt hinges to attach the lid. Install a light hasp on the front edge of the lid and a staple to the front of the box so that the hasp fits over the staple when the lid is closed.

The small outlay involved in making a hot-box will be repaid many times over from the savings gained by not having to use conventional electric or gas cooking.

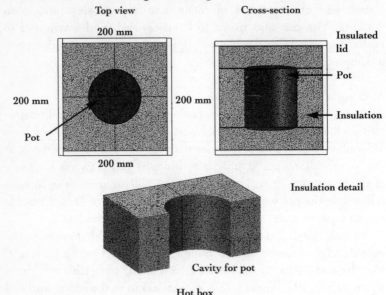

Top view

Cross-section

200 mm

200 mm

200 mm

200 mm

Pot

Insulated lid

Pot

Insulation

Insulation detail

Cavity for pot

Hot box

For a less permanent version of the fireless cooker use an inexpensive styrofoam picnic cooler, or a more durable moulded plastic cooler. As long as it has insulation material, it will work effectively. You can also place insulation material such as hay, shredded newspapers or sawdust, provided it is dry and clean, into the styrofoam cooler. As long as there is a minimum of 100 millimetres (4 inches) of temporary insulation material tightly packed around the cooking pot, and above and below it, your food will be cooked to perfection.

Cooking with the hot-box

Cook the food in the pot on your stove until it boils, or for between one-third and one-half of the usual cooking time. Transfer the pot, with the lid sealed tightly, to the hot-box. Close the hot-box and leave the food to cook for about three times as long to complete cooking from its own heat. You should, however, complete cooking within the first four hours because after this time the temperature of the food can drop significantly, depending on the ingredients and how full the pot was. If you prepare a meal, such as a casserole, in the morning and leave it all day to cook, you may have to reheat it in a microwave oven before serving.

It is important that food cooked in this way is brought to the boil first before being transferred to the hot-box. This will ensure that all bacteria are killed. Food cooked by this method won't overcook, boil over, burn or dry out. If you are going to cook dried beans in the hot-box, you should soak them overnight in water before cooking. Porridge for breakfast can be cooked in the hot-box overnight. Rice, oatmeal, and other grains cooked in a hot-box will swell to their maximum size.

Vegetable herb soup

This warming winter soup is both nutritious and healthy, and is a long-time favourite of my family.

6 potatoes, peeled and diced
1 onion, finely chopped
3 stalks celery, finely chopped
3 medium carrots, finely chopped
1 swede, diced
1 turnip, diced
1 piece pumpkin, finely chopped
3 cloves garlic, minced
bacon bones
3 bay leaves
1 bunch of fresh garlic leaves or chives, finely chopped
1 small handful fresh marjoram or oregano leaves
water
1 generous handful fresh thyme, still on the stalk
1 generous bunch fresh parsley
ground peppercorns, to taste

Put the vegetables, garlic, bacon bones, bay leaves, garlic leaves or chives and marjoram leaves into the pot.

Cover with enough water so that there is at least 5 centimetres (2 inches) of water above them.

Tie the thyme into a bunch with cotton thread, and do the same to the parsley. Place them in the pot with the ends of the cotton hanging over the edge.

Put the lid on the pot and bring to the boil, then transfer to the hot-box.

Before serving, remove the bacon bones, strip off the meat and put the meat back into the soup. Mash the vegetables in the pot and add ground peppercorns to taste.

Vegetable casserole

This winter warmer is not only delicious, it is a highly nutritious, high-fibre meal.

3/4 cup (5 oz / 155 g) kidney beans
1 1/2 cups (250 g / 8 oz) brown rice
3 cups (750 mL / 24 fl oz) water
1/2 cup chives, finely chopped
1 garlic clove, minced
2 bay leaves
1 capsicum (bell pepper), seeded and chopped
250 grams (8 ounces) fresh peas, left in their pods
4 medium carrots, diced
1/2 cup (60 g / 2 oz) corn kernels

Soak the kidney beans overnight, and include the soaking water as part of the 3 cups (750 mL / 24 fl oz) of water to be added to the casserole.

Put all of the ingredients into the pot and bring to the boil. Allow to boil for 2 to 3 minutes with the lid on. Place in the hot-box, close the lid and leave to cook for 3 hours.

THE SOLAR OVEN

Like the hot-box, the solar oven cooks casseroles, stews and soups by slow, prolonged heating. Its drawback is that it will only work when the sun is shining, however, it's a very energy-efficient way to cook a meal, and because it cooks slowly you get the best flavour.

While you can now purchase ready-made solar ovens, it is easy and inexpensive to make your own. Construct a square box from a suitable timber such as 19 millimetre (3/4 inch) ply or particle board. You will need to cut the sides so that the box has a similar shape to that of a salt box — the front shallower than the back, creating a slope of approximately 45 degrees. The front edge should be higher than the pot you intend to cook in. Before assembling the box, the top inner edges must be rebated as they will need to support a double-glazed solar plate.

Screw and glue the sides and base together, then construct a liner from sheet tin to fit snugly inside the box. Paint it on both sides with three or four coats of matt black paint then fit it inside the box. Fit 50 millimetre- (2½ inch-) thick rigid insulation material to the sides and the bottom of the metal liner. Cover the insulation with aluminium foil, shiny side facing out.

Construct a frame for the glass solar plate from 25 x 25 millimetre (1 x 1 inch) DAR timber, rebated to within 6 millimetres (¼ inch) around the inner edge. When assembled, the rebate will hold the double glazing in place. Run a strip of silicone sealant around the rebate then fit the first pane of glass. Make separators from small strips of wood and fit them; when both panes of glass are in place the top pane will be flush with the edge of the frame and there will be a small air space between them. Use silicone sealant on both the bottom and top edges of the separators. When the glass is in place, secure the top pane with half-round storm moulding, overlapping it onto the glass by 10 millimetres (⅖ inch). The glass solar collector is then fitted on top of the box with butt hinges attached to one edge.

Construct a lid from the same timber as the box, to match the outside dimensions of the top of the solar oven box. Line the inside of the lid with aluminium foil, shiny side out. Attach the lid with butt hinges to the top edge at the back of the box. The aluminium foil can be adjusted so as to bounce sunlight through the glass into the box. A far more effective reflective system can be made by making detachable panels lined with aluminium foil. You will need four square panels, each one tailored to the width of the corresponding top edge of the box, that can be clipped on and off. To join them together you will need to make four v-shaped reflective panels, since they will need to radiate out at an angle.

A word of caution: your solar cooker will cause a lot of reflected sunlight to bounce around. There is nothing worse than being temporarily blinded by a flash of intense light, so until you know how everything is working, protect your eyes by wearing sunglasses.

HOME-DRIED PRODUCE

With the wide availability of canned and frozen foods, the practice of preserving food at home by drying it has almost become obsolete. Drying, however, is an excellent natural method by which the home gardener can preserve fruit and vegetables. Nothing is added and only water is removed. With the exception of some loss of vitamins A and C, dried fruit and vegetables contain the same vitamins and minerals as fresh produce. Dried food takes up minimal storage space and is energy-efficient — unlike freezing, it doesn't use up any electricity.

Fruit and vegetables can be dried in a low-cost home-made dryer, a solar dryer, or by using direct sunlight. The most important thing is to remove 80 to 90 per cent of the water content so that bacteria don't develop during storage.

LOW-COST ELECTRIC DRYER

The materials required for this unit are very simple: a topless cardboard box, like the kind used for packing fruit, that is at least 200 millimetres (8 inches) deep; a light socket, base, and electrical cord; a 60 watt light bulb; a metal biscuit-baking tray that will fit inside the box; aluminium foil; a block of wood 100 x 100 millimetres (4 x 4 inches); and a small tin of black paint. If you wish to make a more durable drying unit, you can construct the box from scrap timber.

Start by placing a notch at the top of one of the corners of the box to accommodate the electrical cord. Then line the box with aluminium foil, shiny side up. Cut the block of wood in half on the diagonal. Discard one of the halves and screw the light socket onto the other so that the bulb sits at a 45 degree angle when placed in the box. This will help diffuse the heat more evenly. Position your light bulb set-up securely in the centre of the box, run the cord out through the notch, and place a little aluminium foil on top of the bulb (this will also aid in even heat distribution).

Paint the bottom of the biscuit-baking tray with black paint; this ensures maximum heat absorption. When dry, place the tray over the box, black side down; it should sit a few centimetres (a little over an inch) above the light bulb.

Fill the tray with a layer of sliced fruit or vegetables, and plug in the light. It usually takes about 12 hours to dry the food, depending upon the humidity and the size of the food slices.

Based on current Energy Australia charges, it would cost about 8 cents to process a batch of apples in 12 hours. This compares very favourably with an electric oven, which, at 100 degrees Celsius (210 degrees Fahrenheit) with the door slightly ajar, would take 4.5 hours and cost 48 cents.

SOLAR DRYING CABINET

A solar drying cabinet or dehydrator is easy to build and works on the same principle as the low-cost drying box, except that the heat source is the sun. The average home handyperson should not have any difficulty in constructing the cabinet, since all that is required is a wood-framed cupboard lined with three-ply timber. A solar panel, constructed in exactly the same way as the solar air conditioning roof unit described on pages 68–69, is attached to the front of the unit parallel to its base, and inclined on a slope equal to the latitude of the site plus 5 per cent. There is an adjustable flap on the solar panel to control the flow of air, which is heated as it passes beneath glass panels and into the dehydrator. The hot air passes through the drying trays and is exhausted through an adjustable vent on top of the dehydrator.

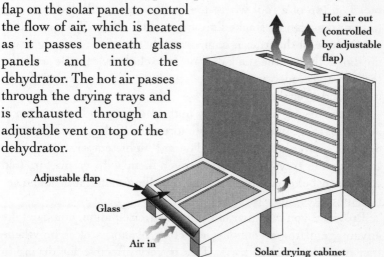

Hot air out (controlled by adjustable flap)

Adjustable flap

Glass

Air in

Solar drying cabinet

Fruit and vegetables are then spread out on trays consisting of wooden frames covered with muslin. These trays are then stacked in the cabinet with an 80 millimetre (3 inch) gap between them for air circulation. The trays need to be removed each evening to stop the food becoming moist again.

SUN-DRYING

The cheapest and easiest way of drying fruit and vegetables is to slice it thinly and place it on trays outdoors so that the sun can dry it naturally. Under ideal sunny, low-humidity conditions, fruit and vegetables will dry in two or three days. But if you live in an area that doesn't have clean, unpolluted air you shouldn't even contemplate this method of food drying.

Construct timber and muslin drying trays. Attach 80 millimetre- (3 inch-) high timber spacer blocks to one side of the frame in each corner. Spacer blocks allow for air circulation. Stretch muslin tightly across the frame and tack it firmly in place or fasten it with a staple gun.

Ideal conditions for outdoor drying are usually somewhat limited. Choose an area that receives maximum sunlight and has a daytime temperature of at least 40 degrees Celsius (105 degrees Fahrenheit). Even though air temperatures at your site may not be that high, you can achieve that temperature by placing the racks on top of a roof where they will receive reflected heat. Up to five trays can be stacked on top of each other. Make sure that the location of the trays is comparatively dust-free. Loosely drape muslin cloth over the stack of trays to exclude insects. Be sure that the trays are adequately spaced to allow air to circulate freely under and over the food.

Set the drying trays out early in the morning and bring them in at night if there is a difference of more than 10 degrees Celsius (50 degrees Fahrenheit) between day and night temperatures. After bringing the trays in at night, cover them with cardboard (old cardboard boxes are fine), heavy towelling material or a shower curtain to keep moisture out.

Provided you can guarantee good air circulation, you can take advantage of the greenhouse effect by placing a clear polythene tent over the stacked trays. This is very effective for drying in areas of higher humidity and lower temperature, but care should be taken in hot, dry areas as excessive heat build-up around the produce can actually cook or burn it. If you choose to construct a polythene tent around your drying trays, ensure that the bottom 150 millimetres (6 inches) of the tent are made from muslin or other suitable netting. This will allow free air circulation and keep the bugs out.

PREPARING FRUIT FOR DRYING

To retain most of the fruits' original colour during the drying process it should be pre-treated. Fruits such as apricots, peaches and apples are best prepared by dipping them into unsweetened lemon or pineapple juice.

Most fruits need to be peeled and sliced before drying. Other fruits, such as grapes, berries and apricots, need to be pitted, sliced in half, and have their skins cracked so that the moisture can readily escape. To do this, blanch the fruit in boiling water for 25 seconds to 1 minute or in steam for 1–2 minutes, depending upon the thickness of the skin and the size of the fruit. Cool immediately by plunging in cold water. Blanch in small batches.

Fruit	Preparation for drying
Apples	Remove the core and cut into thin slices or rings. If the apples have been grown organically, leave the skin on, but otherwise peel them.
Apricots	Blanch. Cut in half and remove the seeds. Either leave in halves or cut into slices or smaller pieces.
Bananas	Peel and slice thinly.
Berries	Blanch quickly or nick with a knife to crack the skins. Halve the larger berries but leave the smaller ones whole.
Cherries	Wash, remove the stems and pits, and drain until juice no longer flows from them.
Grapes	Remove stems and crack skins by blanching quickly or nicking with a knife. Drain until juice no longer flows.
Peaches	Remove fuzz from skin by rubbing briskly with a towel. Cut in halves and remove pits, then slice thinly.

Pears	Wash, remove core and cut into slices or rings.
Plums	Crack skins by blanching quickly or nicking with a knife. May be halved and pitted or left whole.
Prunes	Crack skins by blanching quickly or nicking with a knife. May be halved and pitted or left whole.

PREPARING VEGETABLES FOR DRYING

All vegetables except garlic, hot peppers, mushrooms, onions and leeks should be blanched prior to drying to set the colour, check the ripening process and hasten the drying process by softening the tissues. Vegetables that have been blanched before drying will also require less soaking time when you reconstitute them, and will also have a far better flavour.

The best way to blanch vegetables is to steam them. Place a shallow layer of sliced vegetables (no deeper than 7 centimetres (2¾ inches)) in a wire basket, or stainless steel or enamel colander. Place 5–10 centimetres (2–4 inches) of water in a large, heavy saucepan and bring to the boil. Set the basket or colander above the water, cover tightly, and keep the water boiling rapidly. Steam until every piece of vegetable is heated through.

Alternatively, you could immerse the wire basket or colander in boiling water, but make sure you use a large amount of water in relation to the amount of vegetables so that the water temperature doesn't drop appreciably when you add them. Plunge the vegetables into cold water immediately after being removed from the steam or boiling water.

Use the following table as a guide to blanching times and preparation.

Vegetable	Preparation for drying
Asparagus	Use the top 7.5 centimetres (3 inches) of the spears. Blanch in steam until tender and firm, approximately 4–6 minutes.
Beans (broad)	Shell and blanch in steam for 1 minute.
Beans (runner)	Remove the tips and ends, slice and blanch in steam for 2 minutes.
Beetroot	Cut off the tops, wash well and scrub in cold water. Blanch in boiling water: small beets for 2½ minutes; large beets for 4 minutes.

Broccoli	Slice into 15 millimetre- (½ inch-) wide strips and blanch in boiling water for 3 minutes.
Brussels sprouts	Cut lengthwise into strips about 15 millimetres (½ inch) thick and blanch in boiling water for 3 minutes. Allow to dry until crisp.
Cabbage	Cut into long, thin slices and blanch in steam for 5 minutes.
Capsicum (bell pepper)	Wash and remove stem and seeds. Cut into thin slices and blanch in boiling water for 2 minutes.
Carrots	Wash and slice thinly. Blanch in steam for 2–3 minutes.
Cauliflower	Trim, then break or cut heads into small pieces. Blanch in steam for 4 minutes.
Chillies	Choose mature red chillies and string them together by running a needle and thread through the thickest part of the stems. Leave to hang in a dry place.
Corn	Remove the husk and silk, then blanch the whole cob in boiling water for 10 minutes. Remove the kernels for drying, making sure you don't include any of the husk.
Eggplant (Aubergine)	Peel and slice into thin strips or dice into small cubes. Dissolve 1 tablespoon of salt in 1 litre (1 quart) of cold water and place the eggplant (aubergine) in it for a few seconds to prevent discolouration. Blanch in boiling water for 4 minutes.
Garlic	Peel, then slice or grate. If you intend to use it in soups or casseroles, blanch in boiling water for 1½ minutes, but if you intend to use it for seasoning, do not blanch.
Leeks	Peel, then slice into rings or grate. If you intend to use them in soups or casseroles, blanch in boiling water for 1½ minutes, but if you intend to use them for seasoning, do not blanch them.

Marrow	Do not peel; slice thinly and blanch for about 7 minutes.
Mushrooms	Peel, and cut off the stems if they are tough. Leave whole or slice, depending upon their size. Do not blanch.
Onions	Peel, then slice into rings or grate. If you intend to use them in soups or casseroles, blanch in boiling water for $1\frac{1}{2}$ minutes, but if you intend to use them for seasoning, do not blanch them.
Parsnips	Cut off the tips, peel, wash and dice into small cubes. Blanch in steam for $1\frac{1}{2}$ minutes.
Peas	Remove the shells. Use only young, tender peas. Blanch in boiling water for 1 minute.
Potatoes	Peel, wash and slice into 6 millimetre- ($\frac{1}{4}$ inch-) thick rounds. Blanch in steam for 5 minutes. Mix $\frac{1}{2}$ cup (125 mL / 4 fl oz) of lemon juice with 2 litres (2 quarts) of cold water and immediately after blanching, soak the potatoes in the mixture for 45 minutes; this prevents oxidation during drying.
Pumpkin	Cut into 2.5 centimetre- (1 inch-) wide strips and then peel. Blanch in steam for 3 minutes.
Rhubarb	Cut into strips about 2 centimetres ($\frac{3}{4}$ inch) wide and blanch in boiling water for 3 minutes.
Spinach	Wash thoroughly and cut very coarsely into strips. Blanch in steam for $3\frac{1}{2}$ minutes. Spread no more than 12 millimetres ($\frac{1}{2}$ inch) thick on drying trays.
Squash, summer	Do not peel; slice thinly and blanch for about 7 minutes.
Squash, winter	Cut into 2.5 centimetre- (1 inch-) wide strips and then peel. Blanch in steam for 3 minutes.
Swiss chard	Wash thoroughly and cut very coarsely into strips. Blanch in steam for $3\frac{1}{2}$ minutes. Spread no more than 12 millimetres ($\frac{1}{2}$ inch) thick on drying trays.

Tomatoes	Wash, quarter and blanch in boiling water for about 5 minutes. Run through a mouli or sieve to remove skins and seeds, and then strain the pulp through several thicknesses of cheesecloth. Squeeze out as much water as possible, then spread the pulp out on a metal biscuit tray (if using a solar dryer, the metal tray can be placed on top of one of the drying trays). Turn the pulp frequently during drying until it forms dry flakes.
Turnip	Wash and cut into thin slices or cubes. Blanch in steam for $1\frac{1}{2}$ minutes.
Zucchini (courgettes)	Do not peel; slice into thin strips and blanch for about 7 minutes.

HOW TO TELL IF PRODUCE IS FULLY DRIED

Fruit is sufficiently dehydrated when it becomes leathery, that is, dry and shrivelled on the outside and only slightly soft inside. Beans, peas and corn should be very hard; leafy and thin vegetables should be brittle; and larger vegetable chunks and slices should be leathery. If at all in doubt, leave the produce to dry a little longer.

Some pieces of food will dry faster than others, so it is important to remove pieces as they dry rather than wait until every piece is completely dehydrated. Fruit has the appearance of being moist when it is hot, so occasionally remove a few pieces from the dryer and allow them to cool before determining if they are dry.

PASTEURISING

It is important to pasteurise your dried produced before storing it, as it ensures that no insect eggs or bacteria have a chance to develop. Low heat will have dried the produce, and while blanching will have destroyed most bacteria, it is better to be on the safe side. Spread dried produce in a layer no thicker than 2.5 centimetres (1 inch) on a metal biscuit-baking tray and heat for 10–15 minutes in an oven at 80 degrees Celsius (175 degrees Fahrenheit). Allow to cool completely before storing.

STORAGE OF DRIED PRODUCE

When fruit and vegetables are thoroughly and uniformly dry and have been pasteurised, they should be packed in airtight, sterilised glass jars, or plastic bags or metal cans with snap-on lids. Cans should be lined with clean brown paper bags to prevent dried produce from coming into contact with the metal. Rather than store in large containers it is better to use one-meal size containers, so that if some of the dried produce spoils the loss will only be small.

Place a label on each container indicating the contents and the date that it was packaged. Then put them away in a dark, cool, dry spot, such as a pantry. During warm, humid weather you may have to keep containers under refrigeration so that their contents retain their quality. Occasionally check for mould.

If stored correctly, dried produce will keep for between 6 and 12 months longer if refrigerated. If you find bugs or worms hatching out in any of the containers in early spring, don't throw the contents out. Re-sterilise the food by spreading it on flat metal biscuit-baking trays and placing them in the oven at 150 degrees Celsius (300 degrees Fahrenheit) for 20–30 minutes.

REHYDRATING

Dried produce can be rehydrated by adding 3 cups (750 mL / 24 fl oz) of water for each cup of dried food. Vegetables usually absorb all the water they are capable of in about 2 hours; dried beans and peas need to be left overnight. Fruits require a longer soaking time than vegetables, between 2 and several hours. If the water is absorbed too quickly, add more, a little at a time, until the food will hold no more. Avoid adding too much water, since nutrients will be lost to this extra water.

USES FOR DRIED PRODUCE

Fruit leather

An excellent beginner's project, fruit leather can be made from overripe fruit considered too mushy for drying, or from almost any fruit purée. Process very soft fruit, such as apricots, in a mouli or food processor first. Crush firmer fruit first and heat it in a little water for a few minutes before processing.

To each 2.5 litres (2½ quarts) of purée add 1 cup (250 g / 8 oz) of sugar (use honey if you prefer) and ½ teaspoon of ascorbic acid to prevent browning. Place in the top of a double boiler and steam over hot water for about 10 minutes or until the mixture has reached 90 degrees Celsius (200 degrees Fahrenheit).

Cover metal biscuit-baking trays with plastic wrap (cling film). Spread the purée onto the trays to a thickness of approximately 1 centimetre (⅖ inch), then place in your dryer. The fruit leather is dry enough when you can pull it off the plastic as a whole sheet.

When dry, wrap the fruit leather up in plastic wrap (cling-film), roll up the sheets, then wrap again. Store in the refrigerator for immediate use, or for up to a year in the freezer. To serve, cut with scissors into long strips — makes a delicious, sweet treat for the kids.

Vegetable powders
Dry and pasteurise your vegetables, then grind them up to a fine powder in a blender.

By adding boiling water to the vegetable powder and allowing it to dissolve for 1 minute, you can make an instant vegetable soup. The powder can also be added as a seasoning to stews, casseroles and soups.

Other dried produce ideas
Once you have become expert in the drying technique you might like to try some of these ideas, which include one or two of my family's favourites:
- To make instant soup, drop mounds of bean, tomato or other thick home-made soups on plastic wrap (cling film) and dry into small wafers. Reconstitute in a cup of boiling water.
- Dry small pieces of cooked chicken or beef for snacks or to put in soup.
- Dry thin, flat slices of carrot or turnip and serve as you would potato chips. They make delicious and interesting snacks, especially when served with a dip.
- Bread scraps can be dried and used later for breadcrumbs or stuffing.
- Grains can be dried for longer storage.

- Mint, lemon balm, lemon verbena, rose petals, jasmine flowers, borage, camomile, orange bergamot and ginger root can be dried and stored for use in herbal teas.

THE SOLAR KITCHEN

THE ALAN HAYES COOLGARDIE CUPBOARD

In the old days, food coolers were no more than cupboards with screened or slatted shelves and screened vents on top and bottom letting in cool air, usually from under the house. They worked on convective air circulation and were very popular before the advent of modern refrigeration.

When I first moved to the country I purchased a house that had one of those old-fashioned cooling cupboards. It had louvred vents on three sides and was attached to the outside wall.

I knew that with a bit of imagination I could turn it into something more than just a vegetable storage cupboard. What I finally came up with was a combination of it and the well-known Coolgardie safe, which used wetted hessian walls to keep food cool.

I lined the inside of the cupboard, behind the louvre cooling vents, with stainless-steel insect-proof mesh. I then lined the inside base, roof and door with 50 millimetre- (2 inch-) thick rigid insulation and Laminex to prevent heat gain. A water cistern, designed to work on the same principle as an automatic chicken waterer (a storage tank fitted with a trough around its outside base perimeter, with a small hole at the bottom of the tank connecting it to the trough — this allows water to escape but not to overflow the trough), and fitted with a ball-cock valve to regulate water flow, was installed on top of it. Around its base perimeter a narrow gutter was connected, with three lots of heavy-duty canvas, each one consisting of three layers of canvas sewn together, tacked to each side. One end of the canvas was placed in the cistern water trough and the other end in the lower collection gutter.

Although it may not be everyone's idea of an essential house addition, it is a marvellously simple and effective device for keeping perishable items, such as butter, milk and cheese, cool and fresh. Fruit and vegetables store equally well.

The principle on which the cooling cupboard works is the same as any refrigeration plant: evaporative cooling. Water continually flows through the canvas, evaporates and provides a cool atmosphere around the stored food. The lower collection gutter diverts any water collected through a drip-pipe outlet to anywhere you want it: storage tank, garden plants, etc.

Although an addition of this type does not replace a domestic refrigerator, it does mean that instead of using a large refrigerator, you could use a small and energy-efficient one for storing only meat and frozen goods.

THE SOLAR PANTRY

This simple and effective solar design uses radiated heat to draw cool air from beneath the house and circulate it through a walk-in pantry. A variation of this, the solar pantry, was used by many outback pioneers before domestic refrigeration was available.

The principle is simple. A flue connecting the pantry to the roof heats up during the day from the sun's radiant heat. The hot air in the flue rises and is discharged to the atmosphere. This hot air is then replaced by a cooling current of air drawn up from beneath the house through vents in the pantry floor. As the flue becomes hotter the amount of cool air replacing it becomes greater and the current of air moves faster — an important factor in keeping food fresh and cool.

The best place to build a solar pantry is in a corner in the kitchen or laundry, against an outside wall. Depending on your needs, your solar pantry can even be a large converted cupboard or room fitted out with slatted and wire-screen shelves and storage baskets.

If you are converting an existing structure, remove all the internal linings, insulate the wall cavity and replace the lining. Build a false ceiling over the existing one so that the top of the pantry is also insulated. If possible the door should also be insulated on the inside with a rigid insulation material and then covered with a protective lining. If you are building from scratch, installing insulation will not present such a problem. The floor can be covered with quarry tiles or slate.

Install closeable, screened vents in the floor and ceiling of the pantry. Connect the upper vent to a length of copper or stainless-steel flue pipe with a diameter of 150 millimetres (6 inches), which extends through the roof space and exits through the roof itself. If the flue is located on a north-facing roof slope (south-facing in the northern hemisphere) it need only extend 1 metre (3 feet) above its point of exit. However, on a south-facing roof slope (north-facing in the northern hemisphere) it will need to extend 1 metre (3 feet) above the ridge of the roof, and may need to be kept rigid with supporting guy-wires. Fit a cone-shaped cap with screened outlet vents to the top of the flue pipe. A damper valve can be fitted to the flue inside the pantry; with both the damper and floor vents closed the system can be shut down.

A closeable, screened vent should also be installed at floor level through an outside wall. In cold weather, the floor vents can be closed and the air can be taken from the outside. If the outside air becomes too hot, the outside vent can be closed and the floor vents reopened. Both floor and flue vent screens should preferably be made of stainless steel, or of some other material that will not rust and is insect and vermin-proof.

Milk cartons and bottles can be wrapped in damp cloths and stored in the pantry; the current of air will keep them cold. Even fresh meat stored in a sealed plastic container, with a snap-on lid, will keep well if the container is wrapped in a wet cloth. Storing perishable items in the solar pantry may not appeal to you, but for vegetables and fruit there is nothing quite like it — they remain fresh and crisp for days.

A SOLAR CHIMNEY FOR YOUR REFRIGERATOR AND FREEZER

Refrigerators and freezers give off quite a lot of heat, which can add to the heat build-up inside your home, especially the kitchen. During summer this unwanted heat can contribute to uncomfortable living conditions inside your home. Even if you have implemented adequate measures to reduce heat gain, they will not be effective against heat being generated from within the house. One way to minimise heat build-up is to locate the refrigerator and freezer in a garage or laundry, or on the verandah. However, simple solar modifications will allow you to keep them in the kitchen without suffering from the heat they produce.

Install a screened (i.e., rodent- and insect-proof) closeable vent in the floor behind the appliance and a vent in the ceiling above it. Connect the ceiling vent to a length of copper or stainless steel flue pipe that leads up through the roof. If the flue is located on a north-facing roof slope (south-facing in the northern hemisphere) it need only extend 1 metre (3 feet) above its point of exit. However, on a south-facing roof slope (north-facing in the northern hemisphere) it will need to extend 1 metre (3 feet) above the ridge of the roof. Fit a screened, weatherproof cap to the top of the flue.

The hot air coming out of the back of the appliance will be exhausted up the flue by convection, and will be replaced by cooler air being drawn up from under the house through the floor vent. During the day the flue will heat up and function as a small heat pump, making the system even more effective.

If the aesthetics of this type of modification is a concern, you can build an insulated alcove for the appliances. Provided there is sufficient air space around them, the front of the alcove can be completely boxed in to match your kitchen decor.

6

CONSERVING WATER AND ELECTRICITY

It is so easy to turn on a light switch and forget about it, leave a tap dripping, or run an electric heater all night without realising the impact any of this may be having upon our energy and water supplies. With a simple change in attitude we can use water and energy wisely without inconveniencing our lifestyle.

WATER CONSERVATION

Water is a precious resource that should never be wasted or taken for granted. Sadly, in areas supplied with running water, much wastage occurs. The chief villain in household water wastage is that paragon of our civilized society, the full-flush toilet. No other domestic appliance or activity, except perhaps the watering of gardens and lawns, wastes as much water. A typical user of a full-flush toilet can contaminate over 50,000 litres (11,000 gallons) of pure water a year just to carry away 745 litres (165 gallons) of body waste. There are alternatives, one of which is the flushless composting toilet. However, in urban areas it would be doubtful that local governments would allow its use, the common argument being that it may pose a health risk to neighbouring properties. Yet these units are used extensively in other countries, notably Sweden, who believe it to be the perfect answer to the problem of human waste disposal. There is no water or energy used, no chemicals, no liquid effluent, no plumbing, no cleaning and no smell, and it is an efficient way of turning human waste and organic kitchen scraps, through biological action, into a rich, humus-like garden fertilizer.

Sadly, the composting toilet is likely to be a possibility only for people living in rural areas. There are still a number of other choices, and although they do not eliminate the use of water altogether, they will help considerably in its conservation. One of the best known and most effective ways of saving water in flush toilets is to place a brick in the cistern. This can save as much as 1–2 litres (1–2 quarts) of water each time the toilet is flushed. Plastic bottles filled with water are also effective, and unlike a brick won't damage the cistern if accidentally dropped. A wide array of toilets that include a low flush reservoir in the cistern are now available. They should be an automatic choice if building a new home or remodelling a bathroom.

The bio-cycle septic tank should also be considered if you are not required by a local ordinance to connect to the sewer mains. Basically, it recycles the toilet flush water and automatically pumps it out onto your garden. A sensible modification would be to have this recycled water directed into a collection tank and stored until needed, such as in a garden drip-watering system (see page 138).

After the toilet, the heaviest household water use occurs in the shower. Approximately 30 per cent of domestic water consumption is used in bathing: about 360 litres (80 gallons) a day for a family of four. This can be reduced by installing a flow control valve (available from hardware stores) at the back of your shower head and fitting a water-efficient shower head. Besides the water savings, a reduced-flow shower can also save you substantial amounts in water heating costs.

Saving water should become a habit both in times of drought and times of plenty. In outback farming areas care is always taken to conserve this resource, but those of us who live in the urban fringe should also adopt sensible attitudes.

TIPS FOR WATER CONSERVATION

- Always turn off water when it is not being used.
- Replace leaking washers in dripping taps — one tap can waste more than 500 litres (110 gallons) a day.
- Make sure that hot water taps are properly shut off when not in use.
- Install tap aerators — they are inexpensive, easy to install, and save a family of four about 9 litres (2 gallons) of water a day.

They work by mixing air with the water as it leaves the tap, which gives the illusion that more water is flowing out than actually is.

- Blend hot and cold water when filling a bath. Alternatively, fit a thermostatic mixing valve to both bath and shower outlets. When people shower, a considerable amount of water goes down the drain before they've even correctly adjusted the water and begun to shower. The thermostatic mixing valve mixes hot and cold water so that it comes from the tap at a preset temperature — this allows you to turn off the water while soaping without having to readjust the water when it is turned back on.
- In winter, take short showers rather than baths, and in summer, take cold showers.
- Put the plug in the sink when washing your hands.
- Don't leave the tap running when cleaning your teeth. Use a cup of water instead.
- Use a bucket when you wash your car.
- Reduce the amount of water used in your washing machine by washing only when you have a full load, and use cold water when washing. Automatic machines account for about 15 per cent of the water consumed in households. Washers with suds savers use less water by providing for the reuse of wash water for a second load.
- When buying a new washing machine, choose one that uses water efficiently.
- Soak clothes before washing to shift dirt without harsh cleaners.
- If you must have a dishwasher, use it only when you have a full load — and when buying one, find out how much water it uses. Some automatic dishwashers use between 50–85 litres (11–18 gallons) a day. However, old-fashioned elbow grease will clean just as well and will conserve water.

RAINWATER TANKS

With most water supply authorities now charging for excess water, installing a rainwater tank to make use of roof runoff makes sense. It can provide great drinking water, unadulterated by chemical additives; it can be used for an efficient garden drip-watering system (see page 138); and if it is connected to your laundry it will reduce demands upon supplied water. In fact, a rainwater tank can supply almost all the water you need.

If you're a city dweller and conserve water by collecting it in a rainwater tank, it is wise to purify it before you use it for drinking and cooking. You can fit a water filter to drinking water taps, or strain the water if necessary through several layers of clean muslin cloth, then boil it for 10 minutes to destroy germs. Allow to cool, then add a pinch of salt to each litre (quart) of water to improve its taste.

Boiled water should be used within 24 hours. To restore some of the oxygen lost through boiling, pour the water from one clean container into another several times.

Contaminated water can be purified by adding 20 drops of tincture of iodine to each litre (quart). For cloudy water add 40 drops tincture of iodine to each litre.

GREY WATER

Laundries and bathrooms are responsible for an enormous wastage of water and electricity and for pollution of our waterways. But we all need to be clean and have clean clothes. The solution is to minimise on water use by adopting sensible practices, and to recycle the water that we do use.

As long as you use biodegradable soaps rather than detergents, your laundry, bath and shower water (known as 'grey water') can be purified by simply running it through a filter of gravel, sand and charcoal. Any home handyperson can make a water filter for a very small outlay. It consists of a 200 litre (44 gallon) drum, or other suitable receptacle, filled with alternate layers of clean sand and charcoal, topped with a layer of fine gravel. Inside the tank there is a double pipe system consisting of a large, capped outer pipe which prevents sand from entering a smaller outlet pipe inside it. Water enters the filter through pipes leading from the laundry and bathroom, passes through the filtering material and then flows up the outer pipe and enters the outlet pipe inside, which leads to a storage tank.

For the filter to work it must be sited below the lowest household water outlet point, yet above the entry to the storage tank. Purified grey water is suitable for use in the garden.

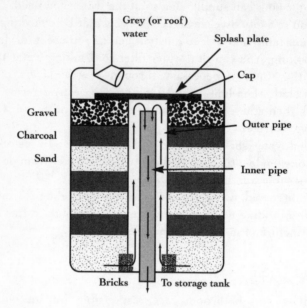

Water filter

ENERGY CONSERVATION

HOT WATER SYSTEMS

Hot water in unlimited supply is a luxury that most of us take for granted. However, it is one area where an enormous wastage of energy occurs. If you use less hot water, you'll save energy.

Don't heat a large quantity of hot water each day if you don't need it. It is far better to install a smaller storage tank that suits your current needs, and replace it as your family grows. When upgrading, install a solar hot water system.

Climatic conditions in most parts of Australia make solar water heating a sensible, practical and inexpensive approach to providing domestic hot water. It is clean, costs nothing to run and requires little, if any, maintenance (see Chapter 4).

Regardless of whether you have a solar, gas or electrical hot water system, it is important to provide additional insulation to prevent energy loss. Although your hot water system is insulated between the inner tank and the outer skin you could still be losing an amazing amount of energy. Wrapping the outside of the heater with a 15 centimetre- (6 inch-) thick layer of foil-faced insulation will greatly reduce heat loss, and is an investment that will quickly pay for itself. Wrap insulation around all out-water delivery pipes — external pipes should have extra wrapping. This can cut power costs by as much as 20 per cent.

If you have an external hot water system, the insulation will need to be protected from the elements. This can be done by wrapping the insulation in flexible aluminium or galvanised iron sheeting, similar to the material used in above-ground swimming pools.

LIGHTING

Home lighting and small appliances can use as much as 10 per cent of your domestic electricity consumption. By changing your habits you can reduce energy consumption even further and save both money and energy.

- Switch off lights if you aren't in the room or if you are leaving the room for more than 5 minutes.
- Use energy-saving light bulbs. If you find their cost out of your reach, choose fluorescent tubes in preference to incandescent globes. Fluorescent tubes will last 10 times longer, use around a third less electricity and will give more light for less energy.
- Keep light bulbs clean and dust-free. By dusting light bulbs on a regular basis you will notice the difference in their efficiency by as much as 50 per cent and will need to switch on fewer lights.
- Install dimmer switches.
- Use a reading lamp on your desk, beside your chair or when reading in bed. (Reading lamps generally use lower voltage light bulbs since they are not required to illuminate whole rooms.)
- Take advantage of natural light by drawing back curtains during the day and installing skylights where you need them.

TIPS FOR CONSERVING ELECTRICITY

- Minimise your use of lights and electrical appliances.
- Check that your electrical appliances operate efficiently. Well maintained and effective door seals on refrigerators and freezers make a big difference. Once they deteriorate, replace them.
- Open refrigerator and freezer doors as little as possible, and then close them again as quickly as possible. Opening the door frequently uses a lot more electricity.
- Check the energy consumption of products before you buy. Refrigerators and freezers have a star rating system to indicate the amount of electricity they use.
- Make sure your refrigerator and freezer have sufficient space around them so that the heat can escape.
- Keep condenser coils at the back of refrigerators and freezers clean and free of dust and lint.
- Adjust thermostats to settings recommended by the manufacturer of the appliance.
- Opt for the smallest refrigerator possible.
- Consider sharing a freezer with a neighbour. Freezers run more efficiently when full.
- Defrost refrigerators and freezers when required; place foods so they are well-spaced, to allow air circulation; do not overload; do not put food in the refrigerator or freezer while it is still hot; cover liquids and solids before storing.
- Don't buy an electrical appliance if there is a manual one that will do the job.
- If possible, repair faulty appliances rather than throwing them away.
- Use a clothesline rather than a clothes dryer.
- If possible, use solar energy or natural gas instead of electricity for heating water and your house, and for cooking.
- When you go on holidays, turn off heating and electrical appliances and the hot water system.

THE CHEMICAL-FREE GARDEN

With the advent of the disposable, throwaway society came the onslaught of chemicals in gardening and agriculture: herbicides, pesticides, insecticides and an array of fertilizers guaranteed to produce super-plants. The continued, and indeed increased, production of these chemicals is without doubt a reflection of the modern attitude towards life — the demand for fast and easy results with minimum effort.

Some gardeners, persuaded by clever marketing, will simply reach for the latest chemical cocktail without even considering the long-term consequences of constant chemical bombardment. They spray routinely as a preventive measure, zap weeds with the wave of a chemical wand, and saturate the soil with fertilizers that do nothing to improve the natural fertility and balance of the soil.

The use of garden chemicals on such a widespread sale is not only harmful to the environment, but also to our health. Everything that is sprayed onto, or added to, the soil eventually ends up in our produce chain: the meat, vegetables and fruit we eat, and the water we drink. The cumulative effect of chemicals is believed to be one of the main causes of severe allergies and other health problems.

However, it is not all doom and gloom. In recent years there has been a huge shift in attitude towards the environment. There is a growing awarenss that we need to work in harmony with it and not against it. Many gardeners are once again adopting the attitude of the past: that a healthy garden needs plenty of added organic matter, and that plants should be grown in areas best suited for their cultivation. The aim is to achieve a natural balance between plants, insects and birds, so that harmony exists.

If you haven't already done so, going organic and converting your garden from chemical dependency is easy. It requires nothing more than composting, mulching, companion planting and natural pest control. And although it may take a little while for your garden to settle into a harmonious balance, the end result will be well worth waiting for.

TAKING CARE OF THE SOIL

The secret to maintaining a healthy, thriving garden is rich, friable soil. Plants will fail to thrive if soil conditions are poor, and will be much more susceptible to insects and diseases.

SOIL TEXTURE

The first step in starting an organic garden is to get to know your soil. This is important, since in many areas the soil is not naturally rich and it may take some time to build up your soil's texture and quality so that you can grow healthy plants. The three main soil categories are as follows:

- *Sandy* soil is light and easy to cultivate, but has the disadvantage of losing moisture too quickly, leaving the ground dry and often hard-caked on the surface.
- *Loam* is the best type of soil to have in your garden because it is easy to cultivate and holds moisture well. A good loam soil contains neither too much sand nor too much clay.
- *Clay* soil is very heavy and extremely hard to work. Water takes a long time to drain away from clay soil.

A simple test to determine the texture of your soil is to take half a handful of soil, lightly moisten it, form it into a sausage shape, and then gently bend it to determine its structure.

- *Sandy* soil will crumble and crack and, if you try to bend it, will fall apart.
- *Loam* will hold together quite well and will form a shape, but will crack slightly when you try to bend it.
- *Clay* is smooth, easy to handle, and will form a shape and bend without cracking.

A more definitive test is to add a small amount of your garden soil to a glass jar full of water then leave it to settle overnight.

Gravel and coarse sand will sink to the bottom and will be topped by a layer of gritty material. This will be followed by a layer of clay.

If the gravel and sand represent the larger percentage, the soil is sandy. The middle layer shows the amount of loam present — if it represents about 40 per cent of the total, the soil is a good loam. If the top layer of clay makes up about half of the content, you have a clay soil.

Once you have determined your soil type the next step is to improve its structure by adding plenty of organic matter, such as compost and manure, on a regular basis. Mulching the surface with similar materials also improves its condition. The idea is to improve the moisture-holding capacity of the soil to more readily sustain plant life. However, if you have clay soil, a clay-breaking substance, such as gypsum, should be added first, followed by large quantities of organic matter.

A quick way to improve sandy soil

If you haven't sufficient compost readily available, every time you water your plants half-fill a bucket with clay, add some water and stir. Once the clay has been completely stirred in and the water has a muddy appearance, dilute it with sufficient water so that it will flow freely through a watering can. Use this liquid to water your plants — it will build up the water-holding capacity of sandy soil.

SOIL PH

The ideal soil pH level for the cultivation of most plants is between 6.5 and 7.0. You can test the pH of your soil with a strip of litmus paper, available from plant nurseries and hardware stores. Press the litmus paper down into slightly damp soil with your thumb. If the paper doesn't change colour, the soil is neutral, or 7.0 on the pH scale. If it turns blue the soil is alkaline, and if it turns pink the soil is acid.

If the soil is alkaline, add plenty of rich organic matter, including peat and pine needles. The latter have a high acid content and as they break down, they will help to create a balance.

If the soil is acid, dig in plenty of compost or well-rotted animal manure, natural lime, dolomite or wood ash.

POOR DRAINAGE

Poor drainage affects the health of some plant species. The simplest way to solve the problem is to add organic matter to the soil. This should improve the texture of the soil, allowing water to drain away more freely. Building up garden beds above ground level improves drainage, as does installing drainage pipes to take water away from plant roots.

Planting deep-rooted species, such as comfrey (*Symphytum* spp.) or lupins (*Lupinus* spp.), in badly drained spots is another alternative. When mature, the plants can be chopped up with a spade and dug into the ground along with lots of well-rotted manure. In the meantime, their roots will have helped to break up the subsoil.

MINERAL DEFICIENCIES

If plants are growing poorly, being attacked by pests, or are disease-prone, it's usually a good indication of soil deficiencies. In most cases these deficiencies can be corrected by the addition of lots of organic matter in the soil, or sometimes the problem can be solved by adjusting the pH level.

The following table will allow you to identify and correct mineral deficiencies.

Nitrogen	Slender fibrous stems. Foliage and stems fade from green to yellow and the plant's growth tends to be slow. Add plenty of well-rotted poultry manure; it has the highest nitrogen content. Other sources of nitrogen are compost, blood and bone, sewage sludge, fish scraps and cottonseed meal.
Phosphorus	Growth slows down, the underside of leaves turn reddish-purple, and fruit trees may lose their fruit early or set fruit late. Add lots of manure, compost and other organic material. Rock mineral phosphate can also be added in combination with manure.
Potassium	Plants grow poorly, leaves turn bronze and curl up, and root systems are underdeveloped. Make a separate compost heap that contains plenty of stable manure and green matter, plus wood ash if you can get it. Spread over the surface of the soil and keep well mulched with organic matter.

Boron	Slow growth, plants become bushy and terminal buds die. Later, lateral buds die, roots or tubers crack and leaves thicken.
	Mulch with well-rotted manure or compost.
Calcium	Thick woody stems and retarded growth, and blackening and dying of roots. In some instances terminal buds and young branches may be deformed.
	Treat with ground natural limestone.
Copper	Slow growth. Shoots and tips die back — this is especially evident in fruit trees.
	Apply plenty of compost or well-rotted manure. Adding rock minerals is helpful; they can be included in the compost heap.
Iron	Leaves at the top of the plant turn yellow. Spotted, coloured areas are evident on young foliage.
	Avoid over-liming. Add plenty of well-rotted manure, crop residues, and blood and bone.
Magnesium	Growth is very slow and plants are late to mature. Entire leaves can become mottled with dead areas, and the spaces between veins on older leaves may turn yellow. On fruit trees watch for patches of dead tissue on older leaves, or leaves dropping, first on old branches, then on twigs from the current season.
	Add seaweed to your compost heap, or 1 litre (1 quart) of sea water to every 50 kilograms (110 pounds) of compost. Incorporate dolomite directly into the soil or include it in your compost pile.
Zinc	Leaves may become mottled and turn yellow, developing an abnormally long and narrow shape.
	This can be a common problem in peat soils, and requires the incorporation of plenty of well-rotted manure and raw phosphate rock minerals, if you can get them.

COMPOSTING

Good soil is the result of continual nurturing and building up with organic matter. Regardless of whether your soil is sandy or clay, or deficient in minerals, the addition of compost and manure will result in a friable soil, and make gardening easier and the results more rewarding.

Composting is usually the best starting point for organic gardening, as it is an environmentally sound means of recycling garden and kitchen wastes. It also one of the most basic means of recycling, assuring that future generations will receive the same benefits from the earth as we do now. Every individual should see it as an essential part of a responsible and efficient home management system.

The principle of composting is simple: if it once lived, when you're finished with it, return it to the earth where it belongs. In the broadest terms, it is the biological reduction of organic wastes to humus — rich humus with a slightly sweet, earthy aroma.

A healthy compost heap needs both water and air to generate the heat required to hasten the breaking-down process. If allowed to dry out, the process will slow; likewise, if air cannot circulate the entire process will take much longer and may even stop.

For a compost heap to operate effectively, it should be built layer upon layer, alternating organic wastes with an activator such as animal manure, blood and bone, or liquid seaweed (see recipe on page 133). The nitrogen and protein content of the activator accelerates the breakdown of the organic matter by encouraging the growth of beneficial bacteria which heat up the heap.

Useful composting ingredients include:

- Leaves — layer them in the compost or make leaf mulch by allowing them to rot.
- Grass clippings — ideal for covering kitchen scraps. They break down quickly and create a lot of heat, which helps hasten the decomposition of other ingredients.
- Seaweed — rinse salt off and chop before adding to the heap. It has the advantages of rotting quickly and containing many useful minerals.
- Rotted sawdust — speeds up decomposition.
- Wood ash — rich in potassium.
- Shredded paper — up to 10 per cent of the total compost heap.
- Weeds — providing that your heap is hot and quick to decompose, weed seeds will be destroyed; the weeds themselves will contribute valuable nutrients.

- Straw — provides bulk and is best added in the form of stable sweepings, a mixture of straw and manure. Cover with grass clippings.
- Kitchen wastes — vegetable scraps and peels, fruit skins and rinds, apple cores, nuts, shells, tea leaves, coffee grounds and crushed egg shells (these will add calcium).
- Vacuum cleaner bag contents and floor sweepings.

To make your compost heap
Clear a patch of ground; remove grass and level the ground if necessary. Compost should always be built on soil, never on concrete. Scatter bricks, placed long, narrow edge down, on the ground within the cleared area; this will encourage air to circulate into the heap.

Put down your first layer of material — grass clippings, garden wastes, kitchen scraps, and so on — in the middle of the cleared area. Next, add a layer of fowl or cow manure, dolomite, or blood and bone to a depth of about 1 centimetre (²/₅ inch). Sprinkle with water. Repeat this procedure, alternating the two layers until your pile is built up. After a week, turn the pile over with a fork to speed up decomposition.

A compost pile about 1 metre (3 feet) high should take about 2 months to break down into humus during summer, but it will take longer in winter. Add the compost to garden soil in spring and autumn at the rate of 1 kilogram (2 pounds) per square metre (per 11 square feet), or a 5 centimetre (2 inch) covering over the garden bed. It can also be used for potting plants, raising seedlings and mulching around growing plants.

Herbal compost activator
To make a bio-dynamic activator that will give you a quick-return compost, mix together the following dried and crushed ingredients:

1 part stinging nettle (*Urtica dioica*)
1 part camomile (*Matricaria spp.*)
1 part yarrow (*Achillea millefolium*)
1 part valerian (*Valeriana officinalis*)
1 part dandelion (*Taraxacum officinale*)
1 part comfrey (*Symphytum* spp.) leaf

Store the mixture in an airtight container in a dark, cool spot.

To make your activator add 1 part of the mixture to 20 parts rainwater in a bucket with a lid. Shake well and leave to stand for 24 hours.

Using a long stick about 5 centimetres (2 inches) in diameter, poke holes in your compost heap, approximately every 30 centimetres (12 inches). Pour 1 cup (250 mL / 8 fl oz) of activator into each hole, cover with soil and leave for 1 month, after which time the compost should be rich, black and crumbly. This mixture is ideal for breaking down tough, fibrous material, soft weeds, grass and manure. If you have only just started a compost heap, let it settle for 2–3 days before adding the activator.

Compost bins

You may prefer to contain your compost in a bin rather than simply making a heap on the ground. A number of commercially manufactured compost bins and tumblers are available but the compost they make is no better than that from a home-made structure. You can avoid unnecessary expenditure by making your own simple compost bin from timber slats, bush poles, concrete blocks, bricks or corrugated iron. The bin should have an earth floor and be open to the air on one side. The other three sides should contain plenty of holes for air circulation. To keep the contents from spilling out, the open side can be fitted with a removable piece of welded-mesh wire.

Underground composting

If you don't have a compost bin or heap, you can simply dig a hole in the garden, fill it with kitchen scraps, sprinkle a cup of dolomite over it, and cover again with soil. After a couple of weeks or so earthworms will have made the soil workable, giving you a high-quality humus.

Composted tin cans

Composted tin cans return essential elements to the soil, and are especially beneficial for fruit trees. Simply crush the cans, spread them around a tree and cover with a layer of mulch about 20 centimetres (8 inches) thick. After approximately 12 months the cans will have completely decomposed, leaving a friable compost.

You can also compost tin cans by crushing them, placing them in a shallow hole, then covering with a layer of dirt 15–20 centimetres (6–8 inches) thick. Keep building up alternate layers of crushed cans and dirt until the pile is approximately 30–45 centimetres (12–18 inches) above ground level. Finish off with a thick layer of mulch over the whole of the mound. The cans will decompose in about 12 months.

NATURAL FERTILIZERS

Compost tea

We all know that composting is good for our garden, but did you know that it can be applied as a liquid tea? If you give it some thought, it makes sense to give your garden a liquid boost, particularly during dry weather when plants are starved for both organic material and water. Most nutrients in compost dissolve quickly and readily in water; by watering with a compost tea the nutrients can be distributed quickly to needy plant roots.

To make compost tea, place a 10 centimetre- (2½ inch-) thick layer of mature compost in a bucket and fill with water. Allow to stand for 48 hours, stirring occasionally, then strain through coarsely woven cloth.

Pour the tea on the soil above the plant roots, or use as a foliar feeder by spraying or sprinkling over the leaves of plants. Repeat fortnightly for flowers and vegetables and monthly for shrubs. Compost tea is especially good for leafy vegetables such as silver beet (*Beta vulgaris*), spinach (*Spinacia oleracea*), cabbage and lettuce. It is also good for bare spots on the lawn, trees that have just been transplanted and indoor plants that need perking up. If you mix a handful of wood ash into the solution it can double as a natural insecticide.

Manure

The reason that manure is such a good, balanced fertilizer is that up to 80 per cent of all the nutrients eaten by farm animals is expelled through their dung. However, the amount of nutrients in these manures, even when dry, is small compared to chemical fertilizers. Therefore it takes 2 tonnes (2 tons) of cow manure to do the same job as 50 kilograms (110 pounds) of ammonium sulphate. Remember though, while it may be easier to put on a bit of chemical fertilizer, chemicals do not supply humus or provide a well-balanced environment for plants and earthworms, which animal manure does.

Cattle manure takes the form of a compact cake. It breaks down slowly so is long-lasting, a desirable characteristic if you want something to feed the soil as a mulch. By comparison, horse manure, being loose-textured, is unreliable as a source of nutrients when left out in the open. Horse manure does, however, produce a great deal of heat during its rapid decomposition, and is therefore an ideal activator in the compost heap. It can also be dug successfully into heavy soils to lighten them.

Poultry manure is higher in potassium than any of the other manures. However, its humus value is poor unless mixed with sawdust, straw, or other fibrous material. Its popularity lies in the fact that, unlike cow or horse manure, it's not likely to introduce weeds into the garden or compost. There is one drawback to poultry manure: unless it is mixed with some form of fibrous material its nitrogen content, in the form of ammonium carbonate, is very high and it can burn crops harshly.

Sheep manure is a valuable, rich source of nitrogen, especially if it can be obtained fresh, before the nutrients have leached out. It makes excellent manure tea, or can be used under a mulch of grass clippings around trees and plants.

By far the richest manure of all is pigeon droppings, which have four times more potash and nitrogen than poultry manure. Also, the phosphorus content is double, making it an ideal choice as a compost activator; it is not safe to dig it directly into a highly productive garden.

Green manuring

Deficient soils can be improved by planting green manure crops which benefit succeeding crops by releasing fertilizing ingredients into the soil when they decay. Green manuring simply involves growing the appropriate crop, such as lupins (*Lupinus* spp.) or cow peas (*Vigna unguiculata*), allowing top growth to develop, slashing it down and then digging it into the soil to rot. This improves the physical condition, or crumb structure, of the soil, conserves mineral matter and increases nitrogen content, improves drainage and temporarily increases the quantity of organic matter entering the soil.

The success of green manuring depends upon conditions being warm and moist enough to allow the rapid decomposition of the buried material. The more immature the crop, and the lighter textured and more aerated the soil, the more rapidly the nutrients will be released.

Green manure crops can be sown at any time provided there is ample water. It is best to grow crops suited to the season. In autumn, New Zealand blue lupins, field peas (*P. sativum* var. *arvense*) or vetches (*Vicia* spp.) can be sown; in spring and early summer, cow peas and Japanese millet (*Echinochloa frumentacea*) can be sown, either alone or in combination. Broadcast 200 grams (7 ounces) of New Zealand lupin and field pea seeds per 8 square metres (86 square feet). Broadcast 125 grams (4½ ounces) of vetch, cow pea and Japanese millet seed per 8 square metres (86 square feet). Sow the seed on prepared, moist soil and cover with soil to a depth of 2–5 centimetres (⅘–2 inches).

When the plants are fully grown, cut them down and dig them into the soil. Sow the next crop of green manure or garden plants immediately, taking care not to place seeds or seedlings in a pocket of chopped-up material.

Wood ash

Different batches of wood ash vary considerably in the amount of nutrients they contain. Generally, wood ash does not contain more than 2–3 per cent potassium, but does include appreciable amounts of lime and magnesia, and also some phosphate. It does have some value as a fertilizer, but should be added only to the compost heap and not applied directly to the soil.

Leaf mould

Bush leaf mould is actually detrimental if placed directly into the soil because it seriously depletes the amount of available nitrogen, resulting in a marked reduction of plant vigour. However, it can be used after having rotted in the compost heap.

Seaweed

Seaweed contains a reasonable amount of potash, and also small quantities of iodine and boron. If chopped up finely it can be used in the compost heap or as a mulch on top of the soil.

Liquid manure

Liquid manure made from fresh or dried poultry manure will give you a rich garden fertilizer concentrate with a high nitrogen content for applying directly to the soil. It can also be added to compost as an activator or used to prepare dug-over ground for next season's vegetables.

It is best made in a clean 200 litre (44 gallon) drum or a large galvanised iron or plastic garbage bin. Quarter-fill your container with dried manure and top up with water. Cover with a lid to keep the smell and flies away. Leave the manure to soak for 2–3 weeks, stirring occasionally; it will then be ready for use.

Don't apply the fertilizer in concentrate form, because too much of a good thing is just as bad as too little. Dilute one part of the fertilizer concentrate with three parts fresh water. Pour fortnightly around flowers and vegetables and monthly around shrubs. It is best to apply it after rain or after the garden has been watered; never use it during a drought without first giving the plants a good watering.

When your concentrate has been exhausted, top up the container with water and again steep for 2–3 weeks. This time add 1 litre (1 quart) of concentrate to a bucket of water. You can steep the manure a third time, diluting 1.5 litres (1½ quarts) of concentrate with a bucket of water.

Once the last batch has been exhausted, add leftover sludge to your compost heap or use as mulch, and start afresh.

Liquid comfrey

Comfrey (*Symphytum* spp.) is a green leafy herb available from most nurseries and is easily grown in the backyard garden. Its leaves make a thick, green, pungent liquid manure that can be used on all garden plants and is especially good for promoting rapid growth in vegetables.

To make the fertilizer, half-fill a large bucket or plastic garbage bin with fresh comfrey leaves, then fill with water. Cover and leave to steep for 3 months. Mix one part of the comfrey concentrate with two parts of fresh water before sprinkling around plants.

The comfrey can be replaced with couch grass (*Elymus repens*) clippings, which also make a good liquid fertilizer.

Liquid seaweed

If you are lucky enough to live near the ocean, you'll have a plentiful supply of seaweed to make into a spray-on fertilizer which also doubles as a natural fungicide for vegetables, ornamentals and trees. Gather sufficient seaweed to one-fifth fill a drum or large garbage bin. Rinse all traces of salt from the seaweed and place it in the container. Cover with water and allow to steep for three weeks, then dilute with two parts of fresh water. Spray onto foliage of plants or apply at soil level.

When the concentrate is exhausted the seaweed can be used as a mulch or added to the compost.

Nettle fertilizer

This is a nitrogen-rich liquid fertilizer which can be used on all plants and is especially good for green leafy vegetables. If using it to fertilize beans, however, only apply it when they first emerge and flowers are set, otherwise they will produce leaves rather than pods.

To make the fertilizer, place a large quantity of stinging nettle (*Urtica dioica*) leaves in a bucket or drum filled with water. Leave to steep for 2 weeks and then dilute — 1 part concentrate to 10 parts water. Use as a liquid fertilizer every fortnight during the growing season.

Diluted urine

If collecting it doesn't worry you, human urine is a good source of nitrogen and your plants will love it. It must be diluted — one part urine to five parts water — and it is essential that everyone in the family is in good health and not suffering from any major medical problems, such as hepatitis.

Apply to the soil around plants once or twice a year using a watering can, or add to the compost pile as an activator.

Bio-dynamic fertilizer

An excellent liquid fertilizer that guarantees healthy vegetable crops can be made by following this recipe:

1 tablespoon dried, powdered cow manure
2 tablespoons dried, powdered seaweed
30 litres (30 quarts) rainwater
1 cup dried dandelion (*Taraxacum officinale*) leaves
1 cup dried stinging nettle (*Urtica dioica*) leaves
1 cup purslane (*Portulaca oleracea*) leaves
1 cup dried camomile (*Matricaria* spp.) flowers
1 cup dried fat-hen leaves (*Chenopodium album*, a wild herb commonly referred to as a weed)
1 cup dried sage (*Salvia officinalis*) leaves

Mix the powdered manure and seaweed with 4.5 litres (4½ quarts) of rainwater in a bucket and stir until dissolved. Cover with clear plastic and leave to soak in the sun for 3 weeks.

Reduce all the dried herbs to a powder by rubbing through a fine wire sieve.

Strain 1 cup of the manure–seaweed liquid and add to a drum containing 25 litres (25 quarts) of rainwater. Add the powdered herbs, stir well, cover with clear plastic and leave in the sun for 2 days before using. Spray it onto garden soil every two weeks during autumn.

Strain the remaining manure–seaweed liquid and store in a suitable container for future use.

Liquid citrus tree fertilizer

To feed your citrus trees, simply dissolve a packet of washing soda in a bucket of water and pour over the top of each tree. It will also act as a natural fungicide and curb black spot. Any leaves that are missed can be treated by dabbing the solution on with a brush.

MULCHING

Mulching your garden with organic matter keeps soil and plants healthy and happy because it improves the soil texture and provides a number of other benefits:

- It prevents weeds from emerging out of the soil between rows of plants and around the base of plants.

- It reduces the need for watering by preventing the loss of moisture from the soil through evaporation.
- Because it keeps the soil slightly moist, it improves its texture.
- It supplies a steady stream of nutrients to the plant roots.
- Decaying mulch builds the soil into rich, friable humus.
  Materials suitable for mulching are:
- Mushroom compost — if a source is handy.
- Home-made compost — suitable for all soil types and conditions.
- Manure — cow and horse manure are the best choice for mulching and should be pulverised before applying to the soil. This can be done by running the lawnmower over the dried manure a few times until it is sufficiently broken down. Well-rotted poultry manure can also be used so long as it is mixed with some type of fibrous litter, such as hay.
- Grass clippings — an excellent mulch when combined with manure or compost, or on its own as a top-layer mulch over another type of mulch.
- Pine-bark chips — an excellent mulch when combined with manure or compost, or on its own as a top-layer mulch over another type of mulch.
- Leaf mould or mulch — can only be used after it has been well rotted. Either add in layers to the compost pile or rake up leaves into a pile in autumn, water well and allow to break down into a friable mulch.

Apply the mulch as it breaks down, maintaining a good deep layer. However, be sure that the mulch layer is not placed too close to the base of newly planted seedlings. You can layer your mulch with different materials to cater for specific needs: a layer of blood and bone at ground level to provide immediate nutrients, then well-rotted and chopped manure to improve soil texture, followed by a thick layer of grass clippings which will keep in moisture and eventually form humus.

A NO-DIG GARDEN

A concept that dates back almost 50 years, the no-dig garden relies on the layering of organic material to reduce the back-breaking work of digging. It is particularly suited to areas with poor or rocky ground. Alternating layers of organic material are built up from ground level. They are never disturbed by any form of cultivation, but simply added to as they decompose and mulch down. Good drainage is achieved and plants generally thrive in this environment.

The first layer can consist of seaweed, kitchen scraps or leaves. This is followed by a layer of old newspapers, then a thin layer of sawdust. It is built up further with alternating layers of grass clippings, manure, compost and chicken scratch litter (if you have access to it).

Seeds or seedlings are planted in the top layer of organic matter, and watered and fed as usual. More organic material is then added each growing season. Like all gardens, it needs to be well mulched to prevent evaporation, especially in summer.

EARTHWORMS

Garden soil that is alive with earthworms is rich and productive. The healthy, strong plants and vegetables in my garden bear testimony to this.

Soil depleted by overuse, excessive chemical abuse, or a lack of organic material will contain very few, if any, earthworms. Their addition to the soil will not instantly give you rich, friable humus, but they will certainly assist in restoring a balance. Combined with added compost, manure and organic fertilizers the earthworms will rapidly multiply, improving the soil over time.

WATERING

Plants need moist soil so that they can take up the nutrients essential for their growth. However, water is a precious resource that should never be wasted or taken for granted. Huge quantities of water are often used just to maintain gardens that are totally unsuited to the climate in which they have been established. The widely held belief that gardens must be maintained to a certain standard even in times of drought, regardless of the amount of water that is used, puts an unrealistic burden on this resource.

The solution, of course, is to change our gardens and gardening techniques to suit our climate. This doesn't mean that our homes and public areas must be dull, it simply means that people should plant trees and shrubs that suit their climatic area, eliminating the need for constant watering.

Many native plants are not only beautiful but also produce edible and delicious fruits and nuts, and serve a twofold purpose: water reduction and a supplementary food source. Reducing the amount of grassed areas in gardens and allowing lawns to go brown in summer, as they do in nature, would further cut back on excessive water usage.

Some plant losses during extremes of dry or wet, heat or cold may not be avoidable. However, siting plants properly, adequate mulching and learning to water our gardens reduces the risk. The only water my own garden receives is that which falls from the sky, except when I'm planting out new seedlings. Yet my plants thrive and I manage to supplement my family's diet with an abundance of fresh vegetables and fruit. This is because I continually maintain a thick mulch on all garden beds, which reduces soil water loss and the need for watering.

TIPS FOR WATER CONSERVATION

- Mulch the soil surface around trees and shrubs and on garden beds — it prevents up to 73 per cent of evaporation loss.
- Water the roots, not the leaves, of the plants. This encourages deep root growth, makes plants hardier, and encourages plant self-sufficiency so that gardens require less watering during dry periods.
- If you have a large number of ferns or annuals, water with a fine spray as this will distribute the water at a rate the soil can absorb, reducing runoff.
- Consider sowing tougher grasses for lawns that aren't so water dependent: Kikuyu (*Pennisetum clandestinum*), couch (*Elymus repens*), Kentucky bluegrass (*Poa pratensis*), perennial ryegrass (*Lolium perenne*), drought-hardy thyme, *Dichondra* spp., or lawn camomile.
- Plant natives — they are hardy and need less water.
- Incorporate hedges or windbreaks in your garden to reduce the drying effect of the wind.
- Avoid establishing garden beds at the base of trees, where there will be competition for water.

- Avoid watering after dark as the risk of forgetting to turn taps off is greater. In summer, water early in the morning; in winter, or in cold climates, water during mid-morning.
- Soaker hoses are an efficient way to water lawns, garden beds and vegetable gardens where plants need watering at ground level only. They provide a light mist of water which soaks in very effectively, especially during very hot, dry or windy weather.
- Low-pressure drip-watering systems are ideal for country gardens where water is limited.
- Install a rainwater tank to make use of roof runoff. It can be used as part of an efficient garden drip-watering system.
- Grey water (water from baths, showers and washing machines) can be siphoned off into a tank for watering vegetables and ornamentals, provided you use pure soap or biodegradable washing products. Not only will your vegetables and flowers thrive with the extra watering, the mild soapy mixture will help to control insect and fungus infestations.

WATERING SEEDLINGS

Plastic bottles make excellent watering cans because you can direct water to the base of young seedlings without knocking them over. Wash the bottle thoroughly, pierce one or more holes in the lid, fill the bottle with water, screw the lid on firmly, aim at the base of the plant and squeeze.

LOW-COST DRIP-WATERING SYSTEM

An effective yet simple drip-watering system can be made from nothing more than a length of garden hose and a rope. Use multi-filament double-braided rope, available from marine suppliers. It doesn't rot and has greater sucking power than conventional rope.

Thread the rope through your length of hose, pierce holes in the hose at regular intervals, and then place one end in a drum of water or rainwater tank. The base of your water storage tank must be above ground level so that water will gradually siphon through the entire length of the rope and trickle out the holes in the hose. This is an efficient way to water the base of plants without wasting precious water.

THE RIGHT PLANTS IN THE RIGHT PLACE

A certain amount of plant losses are to be expected in any garden, but if you are suffering a high rate of loss, it's probably time to question the suitability of the plants you've chosen, and their positions in the garden. Particularly if you are planting a native garden, you may have to face a few failures until you find plants that suit your land.

THE RIGHT TREES

Trees have always been considered the mainstay of any garden, and should be chosen for both aesthetic and practical reasons. For example, nothing looks more attractive in the garden than a lemon tree dripping with yellow fruit that will serve many practical purposes.

Consider these factors when choosing trees for your garden:

- Shade — trees with wide-spreading branches provide an ideal garden retreat for escaping from the summer heat.
- Shelter — look for trees with dense, bushy growth that will provide a natural windbreak. A row of almond trees (*Prunus dulcis*), with a row of olive trees (*Olea europaea*) planted offset, will provide both shelter and a source of produce.
- Privacy — two or three rows of small, dense trees or large shrubs will provide privacy from the street or neighbours.
- Passive-solar energy — deciduous trees planted on the north side of the house (the south side in the northern hemisphere) will allow penetration by the sun in winter, yet provide valuable shading in summer.

THE RIGHT SHRUBS

Large, dense shrubs can be used as a hedge or windbreak to provide privacy and to protect sensitive plants, vegetables for example. Herbs such as lavender (*Lavandula* spp.), rosemary (*Rosmarinus officinalis*), wormwood (*Artemisia absinthium*), sage (*Salvia officinalis*), hyssop (*Gratiola officinalis*), southernwood (*Artemisia abrotanum*) and thyme (*Thymus* spp.) are all suitable for varying size hedges, from 30 centimetres (12 inches) up to 1 metre (3 feet) in height. Herbs will provide colour in the garden, attract birds and bees, and will act as natural insect repellents.

NATIVE PLANTS

Consider planting native plants that are suited to your climate and soil conditions. They provide an attractive display of colour when in flower, require a minimum amount of maintenance once established, and if well mulched, rarely need to be watered after the first few years. Choose species to suit your particular needs, such as privacy and shelter.

Many of the nectar-producing varieties will attract birds into the garden, which help to control insects that would otherwise be a problem. Try to mix different natives together in your garden so that they will be growing as they are found in nature.

COMPANION PLANTING

Companion planting is based on the fact that certain plants give off substances through their leaves and roots which complement the needs of certain other plants. Marigolds (*Calendula officinalis*), for example, repel nematodes. In some instances, the compatibility occurs at a more simple, physical level — for instance, tall plants such as corn (maize) will protect shade-loving plants such as watermelon and cucumbers.

In nature, plant species do not grow close together in ordered rows but grow more haphazardly, according to environmental conditions. The companion planting system follows the model of natural selection, by doing away with ordered garden beds and rows of trees and instead, sowing a mixture of plants according to their compatibility. Companion planting principles can easily be applied to the home garden. All that it requires is a little thought; the results will be basically the same as Mother Nature intended.

Companion planting helps to create a healthy garden, which in turn is less vulnerable to disease and insect attack. It means working in harmony with nature, not against it.

Principles of companion planting

- Shallow-rooted plants thrive when grown near deep-rooted species.
- Leafy crops are best planted with root crops — this way they are not competing for the same ground space or specific nutrients.

- Tall species provide shade and shelter for smaller shade-loving plants.
- Species with different water requirements grow well together as they are not competing for water.
- Species with different nutrient requirements grow well together.
- Some species, such as peas, have roots which give off nitrogen, so should be planted near plants that need plenty of nitrogen.
- Some species, such as garlic, exude aromas that repel insects. Companion plant species are shown in the following table.

Basil (*Ocimum basilicum*)	Repels flies and mosquitoes, and white fly from tomatoes.
Beans	Thrive when planted beside carrots, cauliflowers, cucumbers, corn (maize) and radishes. Summer savory (*Satureja hortensis*) is also beneficial because it repels bean beetles. Beans dislike being grown near onions, beetroot, garlic, gladioli (*Gladiolus* spp.) and sunflowers (*Helianthus* spp.).
Beetroot	Grows well with all plants except pole (climbing) beans, which will stunt their growth. It grows exceptionally well when planted with or near lettuce, cabbage, onions and bush beans.
Cabbage	Rosemary (*Rosmarinus officinalis*), mint (*Mentha* spp.), thyme (*Thymus* spp.) and other aromatic herbs repel the cabbage worm and adult moth. Sage (*Salvia officinalis*) gives off camphor, which also repels the cabbage moth. Don't grow cabbage near strawberries, pole (climbing) beans or tomatoes as they discourage cabbage growth.
Capsicums (bell peppers) and chillies (*Capsicum annuum*)	Onions, carrots, tomatoes and eggplant (aubergine, *Solanum melongena*) are good companions.

Carrots	Carrots grow well with Brussels sprouts (*Brassica oleracea*), peas, cabbage, lettuce, radishes and chives (*Allium schoenoprasum*). Leeks, sage and rosemary repel the carrot fly. Plant carrots and leeks in alternate rows, as the carrots in turn repel the onion fly. Carrots only dislike growing near dill (*Anethum graveolens*), to which they are related.
Catnip (*Nepeta cataria*)	Repels flea beetles and attracts cats.
Cauliflower	Grow near aromatic herbs.
Chives (*Allium schoenoprasum*) Corn (maize)	Chives enhance the growth of carrots and tomatoes and repel a whole host of insects. The addition of nitrogen to the soil by peas and beans enhances the growth of corn. Corn itself stimulates cucumbers, melons and squash (*Cucurbita* spp.), and lures away the tomato pest heliothis.
Cucumbers	One of the few vegetables that dislike being grown near aromatic herbs; they also do not grow well with potatoes. They prefer being near corn, cabbage, bush beans, lettuce or radishes. Radishes keep the cucumber beetle away from cucumbers and all related plants.
Garlic	Repels insect pests, especially from vegetables. Highly diluted garlic extract repels wireworm, caterpillars, weevils, black fly, Japanese beetles, aphids and other leaf-sucking bugs, and protects against fungi such as mildew, bean rust, anthracnose, brown rot and blight.
Lemon balm	Attracts bees and can be used as a border edging in combination with marigolds (*Calendula officinalis*).
Lettuce	Aided by root crops, especially beetroot and carrots. Onions and cabbage are helped along by lettuce growing with them.

Marigolds (*Calendula officinalis*)	Foliage repels bean beetles, tomato fruit worms, flea beetles and white fly. After being grown in the same spot for a few years, the roots of marigolds exude a substance which kills nematodes in the soil.
Marjoram (*Origanum marjorana*)	This herb is credited with stimulating the growth of almost all plants.
Melons	Corn (maize) is a good companion.
Mint (*Mentha* spp.)	Repels the cabbage butterfly and ants.
Nasturtiums (*Tropaeolum majus*)	Repel aphids and cucumber beetles; they also give radishes a great hot flavour.
Onions	Oil from onions inhibits the growth of beans and peas. Onions like growing with most other plants, especially beetroot, cabbage, lettuce and summer savory (*Satureja hortensis*). When planted with carrots, onions will repel the carrot fly, and in turn the onion fly will be inhibited by the carrots.
Oregano (*Origanum vulgare*)	Similar to marjoram, oregano stimulates plant growth in general.
Peas	The nitrogen that peas release into the soil benefits most other plants. Carrots give off a root exudate that benefits peas. Cucumbers, corn (maize) and radishes are also beneficial. Peas dislike growing near onions, garlic and potatoes.
Radishes	Grow well in the presence of carrots, lettuce, peas, cucumbers and climbing peas. Plant nasturtiums (*Tropaeolum majus*) close by for a better flavour. Radishes appear to have no enemies.
Rosemary (*Rosmarinus officinalis*)	Repels cabbage moth, bean beetles and carrot fly.

Rue	Makes a useful edging hedge that insects and
(*Ruta graveolens*)	snails won't go near. Keep it away from sage and basil.
Sage	Gives off camphor which repels cabbage moth,
(*Salvia officinalis*)	bean beetle and carrot fly.
Squash	Grows well with corn (maize).
(*Cucurbita* spp.)	
Stinging nettle	Protects tomatoes from mould.
(*Urtica dioica*)	
Summer savory	Plant between rows of beans as it inhibits the
(*Satureja hortensis*)	bean beetle; onions also appreciate summer savory.
Thyme	Repels cabbage worm and invigorates all
(*Thymus* spp.)	plants that grow near it.
Tomatoes	Grow well near onions, asparagus, parsley, celery, basil, carrots and chives (*Allium schoenoprasum*). Never grow tomatoes near potatoes, dill (*Anethum graveolens*) or cabbage.

CROP ROTATION

Long before chemical fungicides and pesticides came into being, gardeners prevented the build-up of pests and disease by not planting the same vegetable (or type of vegetable) in the same patch of soil two years in succession. Instead, they divided their land into a number of beds and rotated their crops into different beds over a three- or four-year period.

You can practise a simple three-year crop rotation cycle by dividing your vegetable patch into three beds and numbering them. In the first year, grow a selection of the following crops:

- Bed 1: peas, beans, corn (maize), silver beet (*Beta vulgaris*), spinach (*Spinacia oleracea*) and lettuce.
- Bed 2: cabbages, cauliflower, broccoli, turnips (*Brassica rapa*), radishes and kohlrabi (*Brassica oleracea*).
- Bed 3: tomatoes, carrots, leeks, onions, potatoes, cucumbers, celery, beetroot, zucchini (courgettes) and garlic.

The following year, rotate the crops in a clockwise direction around your three beds. This means you will grow the crops of bed 1 in bed 2, the crops of bed 2 in bed 3, and the crops of bed 3 in bed 1. In the third year, rotate clockwise again so that you grow the crops of bed 1 in bed 3, the crops of bed 2 in bed 1, and the crops of bed 3 in bed 2. The following year, start the process all over again from the beginning.

PERMACULTURE

Permaculture is an environmentally safe, self-sustaining system of landscaping and growing food. In permaculture, perennial species are planted together with annuals that readily self-seed, creating a garden that regenerates naturally each season. Crops are not grown in rows but are grouped together with other plants, as in companion planting.

Mulching plays an important role in permaculture. In a similar way to the no-dig garden, the soil surface is regularly renewed with layers of whatever organic material is available. As with all organic gardening, no chemical fertilizers or pesticides are used.

A well-designed permaculture garden can transform a wilderness area into a lush and fertile ecosystem in 12 months. However, careful planning is the key and it would be wise to consult an expert about your garden design before embarking on this type of project.

It is not possible here to give more than this brief outline of how permaculture works. For more detailed information on the permaculture system I would recommend that you consult one of the many books now available on the subject.

PEST CONTROL WITHOUT PESTICIDES

Using organic methods of biological, rather than chemical, control will help you to maintain a healthy garden environment. It will encourage birds, plant-friendly insects and other creatures, such as lizards, to come into your garden, where they will devour many harmful pests.

Pesticide-free pest control relies on your plants being healthy and strong enough to fight off attack. As well as following the general principles outlined earlier in this chapter for creating a healthy garden environment, make sure that you plant species according to their needs — don't plant shade-loving varieties in full sun and vice versa. Don't allow plants to become overcrowded — plants growing too close together may grow weak and subsequently be prone to insects and diseases. It is also important to practise basic garden hygiene: keep your garden free of weeds, remove fallen fruit from the base of fruit trees, and remove any diseased plants.

NATURAL DEFENCE MECHANISMS

Rather than reaching for a chemical spray that's guaranteed to murder every insect — along with many other organisms that live in your garden — develop a healthy environmental attitude.

Make use of natural predators. Your garden is literally teeming with living creatures, all of which create a balance that provides for a healthy garden. Plagues of one particular type of organism only occur when the natural balance is upset.

Some natural predators are easy to see: ladybirds kill aphids; native snails (*Strangesta*) kill common garden snails; and birds and spiders eat many insects.

Encourage friendly species of insects and other creatures to live in your garden and feed on those you wish to eradicate. Frogs, beetles, bees, praying mantis and lizards are some of the creatures that will help to maintain an ecological balance.

Try picking pests off by hand. Learn about their life cycles and attempt to reduce their numbers during periods when they are least active.

INSECT-REPELLING HERBS

Bitter herbs such as southernwood (*Artemisia abrotanum*), wormwood (*Artemisia absinthium*), rue (*Ruta graveolens*) and mugwort (*Artemisia* spp.) will not only repel slugs and insects but also discourage mice and birds from eating newly planted seeds. Dry the herbs first, then powder them by rubbing through a fine wire sieve. Sprinkle this powder over the garden bed and cover with a sprinkling of earth.

Mustard (*Brassica nigra*) is also an excellent pesticide. Grow a bed of it, and when in flower cut it down and dig it into the ground to eliminate insect pests and their eggs. Cayenne powder can be dusted on fruit trees before the fruit ripens to discourage fruit fly. It can also be used to dust cabbages, cauliflowers and tomato plants to kill caterpillars. When using cayenne powder be sure to wear rubber gloves, and not touch your face, mouth or eyes as it burns and irritates for quite a long time. You can either buy commercial cayenne pepper or grind up dried red chillies, using a pestle and mortar, until they are reduced to a powder.

FRUIT FLY TRAPS

Fruit fly is a serious problem in many areas, and can be devastating for the home orchard or vegetable garden. It can be kept under control with traps which can be made easily using recycled materials.

Thoroughly wash a plastic ice-cream container. A little over half-way up one side of the container cut a hole about 25 millimetres (1 inch) in diameter. Make another hole in the same position on the opposite side of the container. Cut six to eight holes with a diameter of about 6 millimetres ($\frac{1}{4}$ inch) in the lid.

Fill the container with soapy water up to the level of 10–20 millimetres ($\frac{2}{5}$–$\frac{3}{4}$ inch). Dissolve 1–2 tablespoons of sugar in the soapy water. (The sugar attracts the flies, the soapy water breaks the water tension so that they drown.) Add a piece of banana skin and secure the lid with masking tape. Make a harness out of string that will fit around the container. Hang one to three traps in a shady part of the tree (they mustn't receive direct sunlight). Empty the traps once a week and refill with the same mixture.

In addition to placing traps, you must never leave fruit to rot on the ground. Pick it up daily and bury it, or if you keep ducks or chickens allow them to free-range near your fruit trees.

The vegetable garden is also an ideal maternity ward for this pest, especially if you grow tomatoes. You can make smaller traps from empty glass jars and hang them strategically throughout the garden. Pierce a hole about thumbnail size in the jar's lid and add the sugary soap solution. Check the traps every second day as they may have to be recharged more frequently.

INSECT BARRIERS AND OTHER CONTROL METHODS

- If possible, inspect your plants each morning and carefully pick off pests such as aphids and caterpillars by hand.
- Badly attacked plants should be completely removed from the garden and in most cases burnt to prevent the problem spreading.
- Try sponging plants with warm soapy water to remove aphids and other leaf-sucking insects, or apply one of the natural organic sprays mentioned earlier in this chapter. Repeat the treatment every few days until the problem disappears.
- The foliage of brassicas (broccoli, Brussels sprouts, cabbage, cauliflower, kale and kohlrabi) can be sprayed with salty water to prevent cabbage moths from laying eggs.
- Plant chrysanthemums or pyrethrum daisies (*Tanacetum* spp.) in your garden as border plants. They will keep the bugs away from your plants.
- Tie large rhubarb (*Rheum* spp.) leaves over the tops of cabbages and cauliflowers to protect them from insect attack.
- Grow garlic, chives and nasturtiums (*Tropaeolum majus*) beneath fruit trees to act as general bug-repellents.
- To kill nematodes in the soil, drench the area with a solution made by dissolving 2 kilograms (4½ pounds) of sugar in a bucket of water. You can use molasses instead of sugar, but not honey as it may transmit diseases to bees.
- Scale, thrips, aphids and mites can be controlled by steeping 1 kilogram (2¼ pounds) of chopped, unpeeled onions in 2 cups (500 mL / 16 fl oz) of boiling water for 1 hour. Strain, dilute with 20 litres (20 quarts) of water and spray on the plants every 10 days until the pests are gone. Spray in the late afternoon. If the solution isn't adhering to your plants, you can dissolve a small amount of soft soap in the mixture.
- To control red spider mites, blend coriander oil with a little methylated spirits, then mix two parts of the mixture with 100 parts of water. Shake well before use. Spray regularly in the late afternoon until the mites have been eradicated, or use as a preventative if the mites are a constant problem in your area.
- Snails and slugs dislike crossing coarse-textured materials, so create barriers using sawdust, crushed eggshells, sand or wood

ash. Another excellent snail barrier can be made by mixing equal parts of lime, wood ash and bran together and sprinkling it around the edges of garden beds.

- Salt sprinkled around garden plants, particularly young ones, will make short work of snails and slugs. Salt can also be sprinkled on any of the other barriers.
- Fold several sheets of slightly dampened newspaper and lay it in rows between young seedlings. Slugs are attracted to the paper and hide between folded sheets. Dispose of the slugs, add the newspaper to the compost and set new traps daily.
- Small circular rounds of mosquito netting placed over young seedlings will protect them from snails and moths. You can make a simple semicircular hoop from rigid wire, over which to drape the mosquito netting. You can protect a row of seedlings by joining a series of these hoops together with lengths of wire and covering with mosquito netting so that it forms a tunnel. Remove once plants are established.
- Make a slug and snail trap by placing small dishes of stale beer or sweetened water into garden beds so they are flush with the ground.
- To prevent the larvae of codlin moth crawling up the trunks of trees and attacking fruit, apply a band of organic pesticide grease around the tree trunk. Make the grease by mixing together 8 parts of powdered resin (available from hardware stores), 4 parts of turpentine, 4 parts of linseed oil and 1 part of honey. Combine all the ingredients in an old pot, bring to the boil and simmer for 15 minutes. Apply to tree trunks while still warm. Apply each season. Leftover grease can be stored for up to 12 months. Simply reheat and reuse.
- Discourage birds from destroying a vegetable crop by hanging aluminium reflectors from strings above the plants. Or make an old-fashioned bird scarer that looks like a bird of prey indigenous to your area and hang it from a line above the garden.
- To prevent birds from damaging fruit trees, hang slices of onion or onion peelings among the fruit. Fine black thread, laced between the branches and among the foliage, is also effective. Alternatively, cover the tree with a net.

ENVIRONMENTALLY SAFE INSECTICIDES

All-purpose garden spray

This insecticide will combat most garden insects, including caterpillars, wireworm, weevils, black fly, aphids and other leaf-sucking insects.

1 cup crushed garlic
2½ tablespoons (50 mL / 1½ fl oz) mineral oil
10 grams (½ oz) soft soap (green soap,
available from hardware stores)
1 litre (1 quart) warm water

Soak the crushed garlic in mineral oil for two days in an airtight jar. Dissolve the soft soap in warm water and mix with the garlic and mineral oil, strain, and then dilute 1 part concentrate with 49 parts warm water.

Spray on plants as required.

Nasturtium spray

Use this to keep woolly aphids away from fruit trees.

2 cups nasturtium (Tropaeolum majus) leaves, tightly packed
1.5 litres (1½ quarts) water

Place the water and nasturtium leaves in an enamel saucepan, bring to the boil, then simmer for 15 minutes. Cover, steep until cool, then strain through muslin cloth, squeezing all the liquid from the leaves. Spray on plants as needed.

Soap and washing soda insecticide

Use this mixture to combat sucking insects such as aphids and scale.

250 grams (8 oz) washing soda
100 grams (3 oz) soft soap (green soap,
available from hardware stores)
hot water
10 litres (10 quarts) cold water

Mix the washing soda with a small quantity of very hot water, stir in the soft soap until dissolved, and dilute with the cold water. Store in a tightly sealed container until needed.

Eucalyptus insecticide

This is an effective, non-residual garden spray that can be used to control earwigs, slugs, snails and slaters.

1 teaspoon eucalyptus oil
2 cups (500 mL / 16 fl oz) soapy water

Mix the eucalyptus oil with the soapy water and spray around the base of plants and seedlings. Repeat when necessary. This spray must not be stored, so use immediately. Wash the sprayer out thoroughly after use.

ENVIRONMENTALLY SAFE FUNGICIDES

Camomile fungicide

Use this fungicide to help destroy and control damping-off fungus and powdery and downy mildew.

1 cup (30 grams / 1 oz) dried camomile (Matricaria spp.) flowers
3 cups (750 mL / 24 fl oz) boiling water

Put the camomile in a non-metallic bowl, pour in the boiling water, cover and steep overnight. Strain through muslin, squeezing all the liquid from the camomile, and spray onto affected plants. Store in a tightly sealed container and use until the fungus has been eradicated.

Chive spray

This fungicide combats mildews that attack members of the squash family (*Cucurbita* spp.), including zucchini (courgettes). It can also be used against apple scab.

1 cup chopped fresh chives (Allium schoenoprasum)
3 cups (750 mL / 24 fl oz) boiling water

Put the chives in a non-metallic bowl, pour in the boiling water, cover, and steep overnight. Strain through muslin, squeezing all the liquid from the chives, and spray onto affected plants immediately. Do not store.

Seaweed fungicide

Seaweed makes a useful fungicide to help control mildew, brown rot, curly leaf and other fungi on vegetables, ornamentals and trees.

Gather enough seaweed to one-fifth fill a drum or large garbage bin. First, rinse all traces of salt from the seaweed. Place it in the container, cover with water and allow to steep for three weeks, then dilute with 2 parts of fresh water. Spray onto the foliage of plants. When the concentrate has all been used the seaweed can be used as a mulch or added to the compost.

Mildew dusting powder

Grind four cups of mustard seeds into a fine powder with a pestle and mortar, or in a blender. Store in a plastic bottle with holes in the lid. Dust onto affected plants as required until the mildew is under control.

INDEX OF RECIPES

Alan Hayes' weekly column, 'It's So Natural' is brought to you in an A–Z of environmentally friendly hints, tips and remedies for home, health and garden.

Finally, a down-to-earth guide to healthy and natural ways to make the things we use every day, from aftershave to throat lozenges to herbal insect repellants.

It's So Natural is about keeping our planet clean and free of chemicals. It is a voice calling for a simpler and better life.

rrp $16.95
ISBN 0 207 18989 7

Alan Hayes shows
you more ways to
save money, to make
safe and natural
products at home and
to simplify your
lifestyle.

Whether you need
hints on a herbal
approach to handling
hangovers, or a how-to
of energy-efficient
home improvements, or
if you just want to
remove a stain from
your carpet, Alan
Hayes, guru of natural
living, has the answer.

rrp $16.95
ISBN 0 207 18823 8

Angus&Robertson
An imprint of HarperCollins*Publishers*

ABOUT THE AUTHOR

Alan Hayes started on his life's path in his teens when his grandmother shared with him the herbal lore that had been passed down through generations of the Hayes family. Widely known to Australians through his 'It's So Natural' writings, it is Alan's knack of adapting the wisdom of the ages into solutions for nineties problems, particularly environmental issues, that sets him apart. His suggestions are economical, easy to use, and they work.

In 1990 Alan began writing a weekly newspaper column of environmentally friendly hints, tips and remedies for home, health and garden. The column, called 'It's So Natural' is now syndicated in well over 200 newspapers around Australia. An impressive list of books soon followed. *It's So Natural*, an A to Z guide to healthy and natural living, and its follow-up, *More of It's So Natural*, were both best-sellers. *Reclaim Recycle Reuse*, which focuses on saving energy by recycling and by using natural products, was recommended by both the Environmental Planning Authority and the United Nations as an essential environmental book for every home.

Alan is married with two children and lives on a small farm property on the Central Coast of New South Wales. When time permits, he indulges his love of ceramics.

WHAT PEOPLE SAY ABOUT ALAN HAYES AND HIS WORK

"This popular newspaper columnist has collected hundreds of ideas for making easy-to-make natural products that are environmentally safe for use around the house and garden and infinitely cheaper than similar commercial products . . . A treasure trove of invaluable ideas that will help the environment and your pocket."

JEAN FERGUSON, *ILLAWARRA MERCURY*

"Alan Hayes is an expert on herbs and getting by naturally."

THE SUNDAY AGE, MELBOURNE

"Alan Hayes is the kind of man you need on hand in a crisis. He's got a cool head, a logical approach and a wealth of tips to save money and stress." *SUNDAY TIMES*, PERTH

"*It's So Natural* is a useful, environmentally safe guide which no family bookshelf should be without." *WEEKEND JOURNAL*

"If ever there was a book that could lay claim to the title of Household Bible, it has to be Alan Hayes' *It's So Natural* . . . This is a brilliant, easy-to-use compendium of environmentally friendly hints, tips and remedies for your home, health and garden." *PANORAMA*

"Hayes presents an A to Z guide of environmentally friendly hints, tips and remedies for your home, health, pets and garden . . . *It's So Natural* encourages everyone to think about keeping our homes and family healthy and happy, and our planet clean through simpler, better solutions to everyday problems." *HOUSE & GARDEN*

"Mr Hayes is a fervent exponent of the natural lifestyle, which was commonplace in past centuries and fortunately has become more widely accepted again now that there is a realisation of the damage done by chemicals to the environment."

SUNDAY EXAMINER, LAUNCESTON